IGNATIAN
SPIRITUALITY

A TO Z

D1488854

Other Books by Jim Manney

An Ignatian Book of Days

A Simple, Life-Changing Prayer: Discovering the Power of St. Ignatius Loyola's Examen

God Finds Us: An Experience of the Spiritual Exercises of St. Ignatius Loyola

What Do You Really Want? St. Ignatius Loyola and the Art of Discernment

What's Your Decision? How to Make Choices with Confidence and Clarity

IGNATIAN SPIRITUALITY

A TO Z

JIM MANNEY

LOYOLA PRESS.
A JESUIT MINISTRY
Chicago

LOYOLAPRESS.
A JESUIT MINISTRY

3441 N. Ashland Avenue
Chicago, Illinois 60657
(800) 621-1008
www.loyolapress.com

Cover art credit: Ars Jesuitica, The Jesuits of Missouri Province

ISBN: 978-0-8294-4598-5
Library of Congress Control Number: 2017948835

Printed in the United States of America.
17 18 19 20 21 22 23 24 25 26 27 Versa 10 9 8 7 6 5 4 3 2 1

To William A. Barry, SJ

Everywhere there is good to be done,
everywhere there is something to be
planted and harvested. For we are
indebted to all men in every condition and
in every place.

—Peter Faber, SJ

Contents

D

E

F

G

H

I

J

L

M

T

U

W

X

Z

Preface: The Ignatian Alphabet

The idea for this book came to me late one Saturday afternoon at a workshop on Ignatian discernment at Manresa Jesuit Retreat House in Bloomfield Hills, Michigan. At the time, I didn't know much about Ignatian spirituality; I was there because I was editing a book on discernment and wanted to learn more about it. I struggled all day to understand what people were talking about. Most were spiritual directors, pastoral counselors, and others who had been part of the Ignatian world a long time. They used strange terms such as "consolation and desolation," "annotations," and "magis." Familiar words such as "indifference" and "desire" seemed to have a special meaning, and people casually referred to the "Contemplatio," "Suscipe," "Examen," and other odd and unfamiliar things. I thought: *What I need is a good little book where I can look up this stuff.* I didn't find one in the retreat house bookstore.

I went on to get an Ignatian education. I went to more workshops, made the Spiritual Exercises, read many books, and learned to walk the Ignatian path along with many friends and mentors.

Over the years, I've met many people who were in the same boat I was in that afternoon at Manresa. Many of them are personally drawn to Ignatian prayer and discernment; they've heard a homily or a talk or made an Ignatian retreat and want to know more. Others are involved in Jesuit ministries and institutions as students, volunteers, employees, board members, or alumni. Some are spiritual directors, therapists, pastors, and others who engage in what Ignatius called spiritual conversation. Some are clergy, lay leaders, and others who make it their business to stay abreast of spiritual movements. All these people—like me—discover that there's a lot to learn about Ignatian spirituality. Like me, they face a learning curve that would be easier to navigate if they had a book where they could look up the terms they keep encountering.

This is that book—the book I wish I had when I was getting started. I tell the story of Ignatius and the Jesuits, explain the main ideas of Ignatian spirituality, clarify unfamiliar terms, and demystify some jargon. I've written entries about the main parts of the Spiritual Exercises; I include some short sketches of famous Jesuits, and, well—look at the Table of Contents. I've covered a lot of ground, eighty-three entries in all, arranged in an A-to-Z lexical format.

The A-to-Z format allows you to read the book any way you want. You can read it straight through. You can consult it when the need arises. If you're beginning an Ignatian education, start with the entry on Ignatius, go to discernment, read about the Spiritual Exercises, and follow your interests from there. If you're interested in Ignatian prayer, start with the entry on the Examen, then read about imaginative prayer, colloquy, and friendship with God. If Jesuit lore is your thing, read the brief history of the Jesuits and then continue to the suppression of the Jesuits, Constitutions, our way of proceeding, helping souls, and *ad majorem dei Gloriam*. As you read, follow the **bolded** terms in the text; these denote other entries in the book that fill in the topic.

The great pitfall of writing about spirituality is a tendency to heaviness and abstraction. To avoid this, I've injected personal observations from time to time, and a bit of my personal history. I've had some fun. (See the entries on Jesuit Conspiracy Theories, Basketball, and Jesuits in Fiction and Film.) I've kept things short. For more, follow up with the books in "An Ignatian Reading List" at the end.

Ignatius saw the spiritual life as a pilgrimage. If you are reading this, chances are that your pilgrimage has taken an Ignatian direction. I hope this book can help you along that Ignatian way.

Jim Manney

Ad Majorem Dei Gloriam

When I was a kid in Catholic school, the nuns made me put the letters JMJ at the top of my test papers and writing exercises. They stood for Jesus, Mary, and Joseph; it was a pleasantly sentimental appeal for the blessing of the Holy Family. Nobody made me write pious letters at the top of my papers in high school, a no-nonsense prep school run by the tough Irish Christian Brothers. But in college, initials reappeared. One of my freshman teachers, a Jesuit, would write the letters AMDG at the top of the blackboard at the beginning of every class.

If JMJ is on one end of the sweetness spectrum, AMDG is at the other. AMDG stands for the Latin phrase *Ad majorem Dei gloriam*, meaning "For the greater glory of God." It's the motto of the Jesuits, and when you think about it, it's a very bold claim. It declares that God is glorified by what I'm doing, even if it seems futile and

3

meaningless. At the same time, it's a profoundly humble claim: the meekest work, even work that seems far removed from the spiritual realm, can give glory to God.

As the Jesuit poet **Gerard Manley Hopkins** wrote:

> It is not only prayer that gives God glory but work. Smiting on an anvil, sawing a beam, whitewashing a wall, driving horses, sweeping, scouring, everything gives God some glory if being in his grace you do it as your duty. . . . To lift up the hands in prayer gives God glory, but a man with a dungfork in his hand, a woman with a slop pail, gives him glory too. He is so great that all things give him glory if you mean they should.

Ad majorem Dei gloriam captures several of the central ideas of Ignatian spirituality—the conviction that God can be found in all things, the desire to find union with God through the work we do, and the importance of seeking the choice that will give God the *greater* glory.

Agere Contra

Several important Ignatian ideas are given extra gravitas by being rendered in Latin (see **Cura Personalis**, **Magis,** and **Suscipe**). One is *agere contra*, which means "do the opposite."

Ignatius says we should do the opposite, *agere contra*, when we're plagued by self-pity, sloth, lust for wealth and power, and other troublesome **desires**. Often you'll see *agere contra* translated as "act against," but Ignatius meant something stronger than that. When you're beset by temptations, don't just pray that they go away. Desire the opposite. Ignatius gives the example of an ambitious cleric who is tempted to seek high church office because he wants the power and creature comforts that go with it. "He should strive to rouse a desire for the contrary," Ignatius says. If you lust for riches, seek poverty. If you want power, pray to be powerless. If you're feeling sorry for yourself, go find someone to help. If it's hard to pray, pray more!

Agere contra illustrates the vigilant assertiveness that permeates the Ignatian outlook. Don't get comfortable. Beware of settling in. Always be alert for the next thing the Lord is calling you to do.

Annotations

When I was just getting started in Ignatian spirituality, I went to a workshop on **discernment** at a Jesuit retreat house with a bunch of highly experienced spiritual directors and others who had been around a long time. I was an outsider, but I foolishly tried to act as if I was part of the club. At lunch I asked a woman when she had made the **Spiritual Exercises**. She said, "I made a nineteenth annotation retreat four years ago." I smiled and nodded. I had no idea what she was talking about.

Turns out that a nineteenth annotation retreat is a way to make the Exercises without going away to a retreat house for thirty days. You work with a spiritual director over six or seven months while keeping up your normal daily routine. It's often called a "retreat in daily life," and it's the most common way for people to make the Exercises these days.

Ignatius described this kind of retreat in the nineteenth of twenty-two "annotations" that he put at the beginning of the published version of the Exercises—hence the name. The annotations are Ignatius's ground rules for the Exercises, written for the director who leads other people through the retreat. They touch on some of the most important ideas of Ignatian spirituality.

The second annotation tells directors to stifle their urge to explain everything and let retreatants figure things out for themselves. Ignatius didn't want the Exercises to be an experience of words and ideas and concepts. "It is not much knowledge that fills and satisfies the soul, but the intimate understanding and relish of the truth," he says. This is one of Ignatius's firmest principles: God speaks most powerfully in our hearts, not our minds.

The fifth annotation says that someone interested in making the Spiritual Exercises should show "**magnanimity** and generosity toward his Creator and Lord." It's often thought that the Exercises are for people with great intelligence, holiness, education, and vast experience in spiritual matters. Ignatius doesn't mention these things. Instead, he's looking for people with a spirit of openness, curiosity, courage, and generosity.

In the fifteenth annotation, Ignatius tells the director of the Exercises not to get in the middle of what's happening between the retreatant and God: "**Permit the Creator to deal directly with the creature**, and the creature directly with his Creator and Lord." This is one of the bedrock principles of Ignatian spirituality. If we look for God, we will find him. We can have a personal relationship with God that's uniquely our own. This idea got Ignatius in trouble: he was suspected of denying the traditional teaching that the church was the mediator between God and his creatures. He was cleared of heresy; it is, after all, Catholic teaching that we can have a personal relationship with God.

The world would be a different place if everyone practiced the twenty-second annotation, known as the **Presupposition**. Ignatius writes, "It is necessary to suppose that every good Christian is more ready to put a good interpretation on another's statement than to condemn it as false."

Arrupe, Pedro, SJ

When you look at modern Jesuit history and talk to Jesuits about why the order looks the way it does, one name stands out: Pedro Arrupe. Arrupe was a cheerful, eloquent, and enormously charismatic man who was **Superior General** of the Jesuits from 1965–1983. He guided a renewal of the Society based on a deeper understanding of its initial Ignatian charism. He oriented the Society toward service to the poor and refugees and emphasized the centrality of the **Spiritual Exercises** to Jesuit ministry. His vision of training **men and women for others** reshaped **Jesuit education** and profoundly influenced Ignatian ministries of all kinds.

Some words attributed to him capture the spirit of Ignatian spirituality as well as anything I know:

Nothing is more practical than finding God, that is, than falling in love in a quite absolute, final way. What you are in love with, what seizes your imagination, will affect everything. It will decide what will get you out of bed in the morning, what you will do with your evenings, how you will spend your weekends, what you read, whom you know, what breaks your heart, and what amazes you with joy and gratitude. Fall in love, stay in love and it will decide everything.

Arrupe suffered a stroke in 1981 and spent the last ten years of his life in an infirmary, paralyzed and mute. He wrote:

More than ever I find myself in the hands of God. This is what I have wanted all my life from my youth. But now there is a difference; the initiative is entirely with God. It is indeed a profound spiritual experience to know and feel myself so totally in God's hands.

Autobiography

In 1552, two of Ignatius's closest friends asked him to write an account of his conversion and the events leading to the founding of the Jesuits. Ignatius was reluctant; he was tired and ill (he died in 1556), and he was temperamentally disinclined to talk about himself in any case. He went ahead with it anyway, and it's a good thing he did. Ignatian spirituality flows directly from the life of Ignatius, and most of what we know about his life comes from his *Autobiography*. It's a rare document—the life of a saint in the saint's own words. It's only about 20,000 words long; you can read it in an evening.

Ignatius sees his life as a **pilgrimage,** and he refers to himself throughout as "the pilgrim." He covers the first part of his life in one sentence: "Until the age of twenty-six, he was a man given up to the vanities of the world, and his chief delight used to be the exercise of arms, with a great and vain desire to gain honor." The tale begins in 1521, when he was wounded in battle, and ends in 1537, a few years before he and his **companions** formed the **Society of Jesus**. It's a literal pilgrimage; Ignatius covered many thousands of miles as he crisscrossed Europe, and journeyed as far as the Holy Land. But the greatest value of the book is Ignatius's account of his spiritual pilgrimage. Nothing comes easily. He goes through spiritual trials and setbacks; doors close unexpectedly; plans fall through. But he gradually learns to open himself to God, who teaches him many things, "just as a schoolmaster treats a child whom he is teaching." In the end, when the pilgrim and his companions find their true mission "to help souls," they give themselves over to it completely.

Ignatius was not a great literary stylist; the *Autobiography* lacks the passion and flair of Augustine's *Confessions*. But the steady, matter-of-fact quality of his writing conveys something of Ignatius's personality. He comes across as a talented man without airs—something of an ordinary guy who thought that if God would bless him, he would bless anybody. You finish the story thinking that maybe something like this could happen to you too.

Awareness

Ignatian prayer is about awareness. It emphasizes noticing, seeing, and visualizing spiritual realities. The **Examen** helps us find God's presence in the routine of our everyday lives. **Imaginative prayer** draws on our senses and imagination to bring the Scriptures to life and make the person of **Jesus** an immediate and powerful reality. **Discernment** sees the inner movements of the heart as signs of how the Holy Spirit is pointing us toward choices that serve God best and bring us a life of joy and satisfaction.

The underlying assumption is that God is active everywhere, trying to catch our attention. **William A. Barry**, SJ, puts it well: "Ignatius presupposes that at every moment of our existence, God is communicating to us who God is, and is trying to draw us into an awareness of who we are in God's sight. He is trying to draw us into a reciprocal conscious relationship." Ignatius found God when he learned to pay attention to his moods and **feelings** and to value his intuitions and perceptions. The essence of Ignatian prayer is becoming attuned to what is stirring spiritually within so that it becomes present to our consciousness.

Ignatian awareness has to do with these inner spiritual movements, not with ideas and abstractions. Ignatius worried that the Spiritual Exercises could become a theological discussion. He instructed the person directing the exercises not to explain things but simply to turn over the material for contemplation with only the shortest summary. He explained, "It is not so much knowledge that fills and satisfies the soul, but the intimate understanding and relish of the truth." Sensing, savoring God is what we're after.

I like the way the spiritual writer Lisa Kelly describes Ignatian awareness:

This experience of being fully present to Christ, or rather Him being fully present to me, stops my mind in its tracks. There is nowhere else to be or wander in to. Here in this moment, with Christ, is the only place I need or want to be. It is where I am most honest about what is going on in my life, where I hear revelation unfettered by the clatter of the day. Only in this full presence is there peace.

Balance

You can often sum up the main idea of a religious movement in a sweeping message short enough to put on a billboard by the side of the road: *Follow the Spirit, Withdraw from the World, Obey the Rules, Pray More, Work for Justice, Live in Community, Live in Poverty.* You can't really do that with Ignatian spirituality. It has a foot in all those camps. In fact, the Ignatian ideal is to reach a state of **indifference**, where all options are on the table and nothing is excluded. The only concern is to do what gives greater glory to God, and that can be many things.

The Ignatian charism is to hold opposing tendencies in balance. In the Ignatian view we must balance trust in God with confident use of our talents; enjoying our community with throwing ourselves into mission; revering sacred things with openness to the world; reflective inwardness with bold action; obedience to authority with hunger for change. One of Ignatius's favorite images was the "pointer of a balance." Think of a child's seesaw in a playground, perfectly level with equal weights on each side, poised in balance on the fulcrum.

As religious images go, the point of equilibrium isn't very exciting. The word *balance* on a billboard along with a picture of a child's seesaw won't stir many passions. But to me it seems like a good symbol for a spirituality of everyday life. Getting through the day successfully usually means achieving balance, not finding "The Answer." It's a matter of "both/and" rather than "either/or."

Barry, William A., SJ

Ignatian spirituality took me over gradually. I waded into the Ignatian waters as an editor at Loyola Press, where I worked on books by Jesuit authors. After a while I was swimming there, and before I knew it I was swimming laps. One of the big steps along the way was encountering the books of William A. Barry, SJ. *God and You* is a wonderful book about prayer—passionate and clear, concise yet somehow touching on every problem and objection I had. Then came *A Friendship Like No Other*. There Barry asks the question, "What does God want from us?" His answer: friendship. He compares the growth of our relationship with God with the growth of a friendship between two people:

> Once we get over the kind of fear of God engendered by early training, we enter something like a honeymoon period with God. This is followed by a period of

distance when we recognize how shamefully short we have fallen of God's hopes for us. This distance is closed when we realize that God loves us, warts and sins and all, and the friendship is solidified. We are able to be ourselves with God. Ultimately we can become collaborators with God in God's family business.

Barry develops his ideas in book after book: Our relationship with God can be intimate; we can walk with **Jesus** like a friend; honesty in prayer is better than pretending; and the big impediment to **friendship with God** is the notion—likely absorbed in childhood—that God is to be feared. Barry has also made a substantial contribution to the field of **spiritual direction**. A psychologist, he is coauthor (with William Connolly, SJ) of *The Practice of Spiritual Direction*, regarded by many experts in the field as one of the best books on the topic. In all he has written twenty books on prayer and Ignatian **discernment**.

Barry is one of a group of Jesuit writers and spiritual directors who brought Ignatian spirituality to a general audience in the 1970s and 1980s. Joseph Tetlow worked in the Jesuit Curia in Rome for many years, and wrote *Choosing Christ in the World,* a widely used guide for directors giving the Spiritual Exercises. George Aschenbrenner, author of *Quickening the Fire in Our Midst,* popularized the **Examen** and became an expert in priestly spirituality. Howard Gray promoted the Spiritual Exercises and trained a generation of spiritual directors. David L. Fleming was longtime editor of *Review for Religious* and author of *Draw Me into Your Friendship*, an invaluable contemporary translation of the Spiritual Exercises.

Basketball

One of the highlights of my college years was watching my school, St. Peter's College, crush Duke 100–71, in the quarter finals of the NIT basketball tournament in Madison Square Garden in New York in 1968. Duke, a nationally ranked basketball powerhouse, was heavily favored to beat St. Peter's, a small Jesuit college across the river in Jersey City. But the Peacocks ran Duke into exhaustion in a dazzling display of run-and-gun playground basketball.

Jesuit schools in the United States have been very good at men's basketball for a long time—and more recently in women's basketball. A common sight during the annual NCAA tournament is the priest standing on the outskirts of a team's huddle during a time-out in a tense moment in the game. Chances are he's a Jesuit.

A colleague at Loyola Press and I once amused ourselves by making an all-star team consisting of alumni of Jesuit universities. In the backcourt we had Bob Cousy (Holy Cross) and John Stockton (Gonzaga). At center was the incomparable Bill Russell (San Francisco). The forwards were Elgin Baylor (Seattle) and Patrick Ewing (Georgetown). On the bench we had Allen Iverson (Georgetown), Steve Nash (Santa Clara), and Dwyane Wade (Marquette). Co-coaches were Al McGuire (Marquette) and John Thompson (Georgetown), who led their teams to NCAA championships.

Why this digression into basketball in a book about Ignatian spirituality? Because basketball is a city game, and cities are where you find Jesuits. The early Jesuits set up shop in the cities of Europe; the countryside was for monks and hermits. The Jesuits have been in the cities ever since. Most of the twenty-eight Jesuit colleges and universities in the United States are located in urban areas, often right downtown. Basketball is a game of constant motion; it blends teamwork, individual skills, improvisation, and finesse. If you want a metaphor for Ignatian spirituality, basketball is a good one.

Boldness

Early on I was struck by the boldness of Ignatian spirituality. The question posed in the Spiritual Exercises is "What ought I *do* for Christ?" and we're not to be shy about seeking an answer. Ignatius repeatedly counsels those making the Exercises to ask God for what they want. When obstacles appear, you're to confront them, following the principle of ***agere contra***—do the opposite. If you don't feel like praying, pray more; if you're drawn to riches, give some money away; if you can't stand your annoying coworker, spend some more time with them.

Ignatius wasn't much inclined to sit around and wait for things to happen. He told a Jesuit complaining about dryness of soul that "it may easily come from a lack of confidence, or faintheartedness and, consequently, can be cured by the contrary." He wrote to Jesuits in Portugal: "No commonplace achievement will satisfy the great obligations you have of excelling." Boldness is a big part of the way the Jesuits see themselves. "A holy boldness, 'a certain apostolic aggressivity,' is typical of **our way of proceeding**," the Thirty-Fourth General Congregation said in 1995.

Ignatian boldness is guided by **discernment** and it's tempered by habits of reflective attention. The Jesuit writer David L. Fleming says that the tenor of Ignatian spirituality is "active passivity." It's a typically Ignatian "both/and" paradox, something I came to see as characteristic of Ignatian spirituality as well.

———

The Call of the King

The Call of the King is the first of several meditations in the second week of the **Spiritual Exercises** that guide a person toward a decision about how best to serve God. It's an imaginative exercise, like many others in the Spiritual Exercises. Ignatius presents a situation and asks us to think about how we respond to it.

Imagine that a powerful and terrifically charismatic earthly king has invited you to join him in a project to overcome the evils that afflict the world. It's a personal invitation; the king is inviting *you* to help him do something wonderful. How would you respond? Ignatius assumes that every sensible person would sign on gladly.

Now the scene changes; the King is Christ, and the work you're asked to do is nothing less than Christ's work of healing the world. Christ's invitation is a call to work *with* him: "Whoever wishes to join me in this mission must be willing to labor with me," Christ says. You'll be working alongside Christ. **Work** isn't just work; it's a way to draw closer to Christ, to know him intimately, to be one with him. Christ *needs* you. Christ speaks to *you* personally, not just as someone in the crowd. Christ *beckons* to you; he *wants* you to join him. He hopes you will say yes.

You might answer this call in a couple of different ways. One is the "reasonable" response: "Sure, I'll sign up. Who wouldn't?" If you were eager to join the earthly king, you would probably join Christ with even more energy and enthusiasm. But you could go further. You might become one of those people who "offer themselves entirely for the work," as Ignatius puts it. Ignatius goes even further than "entirely." He speaks of people who will "give greater proof of their love" by acting against their natural inclinations to "make offerings of greater value." People who want this will ask to be chosen to endure the poverty and rejection that Christ suffered so that they can give all they have.

This exceptional effort is the famous ***magis*** of Ignatian spirituality. *Magis* is a Latin word meaning "more." This yearning to reach greater heights, to conquer new frontiers, to hold nothing back is the possible response that the Call of the King exercise holds up for our consideration.

Cardoner Vision

In 1522, not long after his conversion, Ignatius sat praying on the bank of the Cardoner River near the village of Manresa in northern Spain. In his *Autobiography*, he describes an extraordinary vision:

> He sat down for a little while with his face to the river—Cardoner—which was running deep. While he was seated there, the eyes of his understanding began to be opened; though he did not see any vision, he understood and knew many things, both spiritual things and matters of faith and learning, and this was with so great an enlightenment that everything seemed new to him. It was as if he were a new man with a new intellect.

We don't know for sure what happened. Ignatius often said that the vision was a pivotal event but he didn't say why, leaving it up to others to speculate. It's been noted that, soon after the vision, Ignatius abandoned severe fasting and harsh penitential practices, and embraced a more **balanced** spirituality. Juan Polanco, his secretary, said that the Cardoner vision led directly to his decision to write the Spiritual Exercises. Many Ignatian scholars think that the vision is the basis for the **Contemplation to Attain the Love of God** at the end of the Spiritual Exercises. The Contemplation certainly has mystical overtones; it presents God, who is present in all things, who labors to transform creation, and who bathes all of creation in a ceaseless flow of blessings and gifts, like the sunlight emanating from the sun.

The Ignatian tradition regards the Cardoner vision as a turning point in Ignatius's life and ministry. It's a reminder that Ignatius was a mystic as well as a learned intellectual, and that much of what he knew came directly from God.

Colloquy

Colloquy is one of the methods of Ignatian prayer that I like best. It is prayer in the form of a heartfelt, free-flowing **conversation**; colloquies are made "by speaking exactly as one friend speaks to another," Ignatius writes. The Spiritual Exercises are full of colloquies with Jesus, Mary, and God the Father. A typical colloquy is about "extolling the mercy of God our Lord, pouring out my thoughts to Him, and giving thanks to Him that up to this very moment He has granted me life." In another, "I will beg for grace to follow and imitate more closely our Lord, who has just become man for me."

In a colloquy we speak and listen as the Spirit moves us, expressing ourselves as a friend speaks to a friend. As in any meaningful conversation, it's important to listen. When you pray a colloquy, talk to the Lord like a friend, but leave plenty of time for silent listening.

Companions

Ignatius began to look for friends as soon as he was converted. He had a gift for friendship; at the University of Paris he made many friends, students like himself, and six of them were the companions who were the nucleus of the Jesuits. The best-known are **Francis Xavier**, a Basque like Ignatius, and **Peter Faber**, from Savoy. The others were Simão Rodrigues, a Portuguese, and the Spaniards Diego Laínez, Alfonso Salmerón, and Nicolás de Bobadilla. In 1534, these seven made vows of poverty and chastity and resolved to serve God together. Later they were joined by Claude Le Jay, a Savoyard friend of Faber, Paschase Broet of Picardy, and Jean Codure of Dauphiné. These were the ten men who constituted the **Society of Jesus** when Pope Paul III confirmed it on September 27, 1540.

Ignatius and his companions became "friends in the Lord," who thought of themselves as a group like the disciples of Christ. They shared a common spiritual experience and gradually came to a common decision to serve God together. Ignatius is regarded as the founder of the Jesuits, but he was really only the first among equals. In reality, the Jesuits came from a process of communal **discernment** and **decision making**.

Companionship is an important part of the Ignatian outlook. People make the Exercises with the help of a spiritual director, who is essentially a trusted companion. **Colloquy**, **imaginative prayer**, the **Examen**, and other forms of Ignatian prayer are meant to foster a warm personal relationship with **Jesus**. Ignatian ministry is rarely done by individuals acting alone. It's a work of "friends in the Lord."

Consolation and Desolation

If you practice Ignatian **discernment**, or if you experience Ignatian **spiritual direction**, you will spend a lot of time perceiving and interpreting inner states of feeling called consolation and desolation. This can get complicated. Ignatius formulated twenty-two **rules for the discernment of spirits**, and over the years they've been supplemented by a great mound of commentary, some of it quite technical. So it's important to recognize at the start that consolation and desolation are familiar to all of us. We all know the joy and confidence that come with being connected to God and to other people. We also know the pain and sadness that well up when we're alienated from our true selves and others. When I was learning about these ideas, it helped a lot when I realized that consolation and desolation were familiar to me even though the words were not.

Consolation is "every increase of faith, hope, and love, and all interior joy that invites and attracts to what is heavenly," according to Ignatius. The early Jesuit **Jerome Nadal** described consolation as "an inner joy, a serenity in judgment, a relish, a light, a reassuring step forward, a clarification of insight." Consolation is the work of the Holy Spirit. The aim of spiritual direction is to help people live in a state of consolation. In discernment, consolation is a sign that you're heading the right direction.

Desolation is the opposite. Ignatius says that it's "darkness of soul, turmoil of spirit, inclination to what is low and earthly, restlessness rising from many disturbances and temptations which lead to want of faith, want of hope, want of love." Desolation is produced by **the evil spirit,** who seeks to separate us from God. Desolation is not an uncommon experience. In fact, fourteen of Ignatius's rules for the discernment of spirits are about preparing for, coping with, and fending off desolation.

Consolation and desolation involve **feelings**—often strong ones. Consolation usually brings positive emotions, such as peace, joy, satisfaction, and confidence. Desolation brings the opposite—anxiety, alienation, fear, and other negative feelings. But consolation and desolation aren't simply feelings (here's where it starts to get complicated): they are spiritual states. Consolation isn't simply feeling good, and desolation isn't just feeling bad. They are about moving toward God and moving away from him.

For example, someone praises you for a job well done. You will probably feel pretty good about this, but those feelings aren't consolation. But perhaps the praise causes you to feel profound **gratitude**. You're thankful for the work you do, for the people you work with. This is consolation. It's a spiritual movement deep within that's produced by the Holy Spirit. The movement could go in the other direction too. The praise you receive might make you proud. You think you're finally getting some long-overdue credit. You're glad that others can see how important you are. This line of thinking can alienate you from other people and from God. It's desolation produced by **the evil spirit**.

The example shows how tricky it can be to identify consolation and desolation. Feelings are a good indicator, but you can be in consolation while you're feeling bad and desolation while you're feeling good. A Jesuit once gave me a good rule of thumb: Look at the direction of the feeling. Is it helping you appreciate God's gifts? Does it tend to draw you closer to other people? Chances are it's consolation. Is it drawing you away from others? Are your thoughts mainly about yourself? Then it's likely to be desolation.

Constitutions

Ignatius spent fifteen years writing Constitutions that set out the way in which the **Society of Jesus** should conduct itself. It's a big book: thousands of words in ten chapters covering everything from the Society's mission and governance to the way Jesuits should behave when they are ill ("in their illnesses all should try to draw fruit from them, not only for themselves but for the edification of others"). Hardly anyone outside the Jesuits reads the Constitutions (and I'll bet few inside the Society spend much time with them either). That's a shame, because they are full of wisdom that everyone, not just Jesuits, can learn from.

Take what it says about mission, for example. When choosing where to work, priority should go to places where the need is greatest and where "greater fruit is likely to be reaped." Ignatius wants superiors to look for mission opportunities where Jesuits can influence people who in turn can influence others, commenting that "the more universal the good, the more it is divine." At the same time, he directed that preference be given to places where no one else is taking care of needs, and to places where **the evil spirit** is especially active. The central image of the Jesuit disciple is that of a laborer in the vineyard of the Lord.

Two phrases crop up time and again. "**Helping souls**" is the Jesuit mission; love of God and love of neighbor are inextricably linked. The other is *discreta caritas*—discerning love, a classic Ignatian idea. Love is unlimited but it should be discerning—purified of **disordered affections**. Ignatius wants this love and service to be personal. He specifies some of these works in the Constitutions: "assistance to the sick, especially in hospitals"; "the reconciliation of quarrelling parties"; "doing what they can for the poor and for prisoners in the jails, both personally and getting others to do so."

The Constitutions are full of norms and regulations, but Ignatius almost always qualifies the rules and is careful to leave lots of room for a flexible application. He continually reminds superiors to pay attention to "times, places, circumstances, and the person involved."

Contemplation to Attain
the Love of God

The **Spiritual Exercises** end with a meditation on God that Ignatius calls the Contemplation to Attain the Love of God. In Ignatian circles you'll often hear it referred to as the *Contemplatio*. Some experts think that it comes from the **Cardoner Vision**, a mystical event that was a turning point in Ignatius's life. It's one of the most important Ignatian texts because it expresses better than anything else how Ignatius understood God. In a sense, everything flows from it.

The Contemplation focuses on four of God's attributes: his generosity to each of us personally; his presence in all things; his energetic activity in the world; and his ceaseless giving of blessings and gifts. There's nothing here about God as judge or one who sets demanding standards of behavior. There's nothing here about God as the all-powerful, almighty Lord of the universe. God has these attributes (and others we cannot imagine), but Ignatius isn't concerned with them. He wants us to think of God as personal, present, accessible, urgently inviting us into relationship.

The Contemplation begins by seeing God as radically present in our world.

> This is to reflect how God dwells in creatures: in the elements giving them existence, in the plants giving them life, in the animals conferring upon them sensation, in man bestowing understanding.

This sense of God's presence in the world is summed up in the phrase **finding God in all things**. If you're looking for the beating heart of Ignatian spirituality, here it is. When I explain Ignatian spirituality to someone who knows nothing about it, I begin here: it's a spiritual perspective that sees God as present in *all* things, not just in "holy" things. We find God *here*, not *out there*. We can't exhaust "all things." God is always present in new ways. This is why Ignatian spirituality is at home in all the aspects of human culture. "Christ is found in ten thousand places," says the Jesuit poet **Gerard Manley Hopkins**.

The Contemplation continues:

> Consider how God works and labors for me in all creatures upon the face of the earth, that is, He conducts

Himself as one who labors. Thus, in the heavens, the elements, the plants, the fruits, the cattle, etc., He gives being, conserves them, confers life and sensation.

God is the creative power sustaining and healing the world, laboring to make it better. In **The Call of the King** meditation in the Spiritual Exercises, Ignatius imagines Christ inviting each of us to join him, to "work with me by day and watch with me by night." We get to know Christ by working with him. The Ignatian way is a way of **work**.

The Contemplation ends with God as the infinitely generous giver of gifts:

This is to consider all blessings and gifts as descending from above. Thus, my limited power comes from the supreme and infinite power above, and so, too, justice, goodness, mercy, etc., descend from above as the rays of light descend from the sun, and as the waters flow from their fountains.

God is like the sun and his gifts are like sunshine. He's not stingy, as some imagine him, but generous beyond all imagining. He's not merely present, but *abundantly* present. As St. Thérèse of Lisieux said, "Everything is grace."

Contemplative in Action

For years I was a blogger and writer on the team responsible for the digital ministries of Loyola Press. One day we took a look at the popularity of Google searches for Ignatian terms so that we could get an idea of what people were interested in. Lots of people searched for information about **Spiritual Exercises** and **discernment**—no surprise there. But we were mildly surprised to discover that "contemplative in action" was a popular search term. It's a bit of Ignatian inside baseball that has struck a chord.

The term was coined by **Jerome Nadal**, one of Ignatius's closest associates, who applied it to Ignatius himself. He was, Nadal said, a "contemplative in action" and "in all things, actions, conversations, he felt and contemplated the presence of God and the attraction of spiritual things." Jesuits seized on Nadal's phrase; it brought together two aspects of their call that are in tension—their mission-centered apostolic work, and their desire to always be in tune with the movements of the Spirit. They would be "contemplatives in action."

The phrase is frequently misunderstood. A contemplative in action isn't a busy person who also prays a lot, or a pious person who's very busy. The Latin phrase that Nadal used to describe Ignatius is *contemplativus simul in actione*, which means "contemplative at the same time as in action." This is someone who can continually reflect on God's presence *while* they are fully engaged in the affairs of the world. That's hard to do.

William A. Barry, SJ, compares the kind of relationship that a contemplative in action has with God to a deep friendship between two people. "They are aware of each other even when they are apart or not engaging directly with each other," he writes. "Although they may not be talking, at some deep level they are in touch with each other."

Conversation

I spent my junior year of college living with the Jesuits at Campion Hall at Oxford University. The British Jesuits were talkers. Witty talk, learned talk, meandering digressive talk, small talk, and, often enough, spiritual talk. They're not unique. When you hang out with Jesuits, expect a lot of talk. It's almost as if Ignatius, in moving away from the silent, monastic model of religious life, wanted his men to talk as much as they could.

That's actually not far from the truth; conversation was a deliberate evangelistic strategy for Ignatius. He thought that the usual ways of helping people into a relationship with Christ—reading books, listening to sermons, praying devotions—were too passive. He wanted a more active style of ministry that suited people living busy lives. He described his ministry with the Spanish word *conversar*. It means "converse," but more broadly it means "deal with" or "interact with." It's an active sharing of grace and gifts.

Jerome Nadal, a leader of the early Jesuits, applauded "the conversational disciple." This person would "quietly and slowly win over his neighbor, to deal with him gently and light the flame of charity in his heart." Nadal said that Ignatius was a master of conversation. "Even though the person in question was a hardened sinner, he found something in him to love," Nadal said. Ignatius would start a conversation and look for an opportunity to give it a spiritual turn. Ignatius called this method "entering by their door so as to come out by our door."

Ignatius cared about the way Jesuits talked. He told Jesuits participating in the Council of Trent to adjust their tone: "In discussions and arguments it is well to be brief; in order, however, to get men to follow virtue and to flee from vice, your speech should be long, and full of charity and kindness." Centuries before hacked e-mails, he warned his men to be prudent in conversation. "Do not think you are talking in private, but in public. Say nothing you would not wish everyone to know."

Cristo Rey Network

The Cristo Rey Network is a Jesuit-flavored association of Catholic college prep schools that has had great success serving economically disadvantaged students. The schools are known for an innovative funding approach whereby students earn most of their tuition through employment in a corporate work-study program throughout the school year. Jesuits in Chicago developed the Cristo Rey model and opened the first Cristo Rey school in 1996. About a third of the schools in the network are Jesuit-affiliated.

In 2017, nearly 11,000 students were enrolled in thirty-two Cristo Rey schools in twenty-one states. The schools serve young people of color from low-income families. About 90 percent of Cristo Rey graduates go on to college. The Jesuits are rightly proud of the Cristo Rey model, which testifies to a tradition of innovation in **Jesuit education** from the sixteenth century to the present day.

Cura Personalis

Cura Personalis is a Latin phrase that means "care of the entire person." It's the way Jesuits are supposed to treat one another and those they serve. The motto *cura personalis* isn't old; the Superior General of the Jesuits first used it in a letter in 1951, in which he told provincial superiors to take a personal concern for the welfare of individual Jesuits when making assignments to schools and other ministries. (Yes, the Jesuits wrote to each other in Latin as recently as the 1950s.)

The idea of personal care goes back to the beginning of the Society in the sixteenth century. Religious life at the time was hard on people. The idea was that you could elevate the spirit by subduing the body with stringent fasts and severe penances. Ignatius rejected this idea. There were practical considerations—Jesuits were engaged in active ministry all day long; they couldn't do their work if they abused their bodies. Ignatius was also skeptical about the supposed spiritual benefits of harsh self-denial. In a letter to a Jesuit with a taste for such things, he listed four reasons why extreme penances are bad for you: (1) you wear yourself out and make others care for you; (2) gains achieved this way often don't last; (3) you burn out and abandon your vocation; and (4) you become too weak to practice virtue. Ignatius insisted that Jesuits eat well, get adequate rest, take time for relaxation, and generally observe a **balanced** style of life. Jesuits have generally followed this policy ever since. They are not known for penitential practices and self-denial.

This anti-ascetic tradition is the theme of a good Jesuit joke with many iterations. Here's one popular version: A young man thinking about joining the Jesuits is invited for dinner at the local Jesuit residence, a large home in an upscale part of town. He admires the plush carpets and expensive furniture. He has a cocktail with the priests, then sits down for a splendid dinner with an appetizer, wine, a steak entrée, and crème brûlée for dessert. Afterward, he's asked if he would like to be a Jesuit. "Yes," he says. "If this is poverty, I can't wait for chastity."

Decision Making

We've all made some bad decisions. This shouldn't be surprising. Cognitive scientists have compiled a long list of the biases, mistakes, and irrational assumptions we make when it comes to making decisions. We think we have more control over situations than we actually do; we prefer small immediate benefits to greater long-term benefits; we underestimate the time and effort a project will take; we see patterns in past events when none actually exist; when good things happen, we take the credit; when things go bad, we're not to blame. The biggest problem is "confirmation bias." When it's time for a decision, most people have a good idea of what they want to do, and will systematically look for reasons to do it and ignore reasons not to. It's almost as if it's an accident when a decision turns out well.

Ignatius knew all about the self-serving irrationalities and biases that fog up decision making. He said that the most important thing is to be clear about the goal; we should see our decisions as a means of loving and serving God. Many times we have it backwards; we make God a means to our decisions. We choose something—a relationship, a career, a style of life—and then ask God to make it happen. Ignatius said that the person making the decision should be willing to pray, to weigh factors carefully, to achieve self-knowledge, and to strive to be free of **disordered affections**. Ignatius assumes that the person can use the tools of Ignatian **discernment**. This implies that the person making the decision is discussing the matter with another person who can give sound spiritual counsel.

Ignatius says that there are three circumstances in which we make decisions:

When there's no doubt about it.

On occasion, God makes the choice unmistakably clear. Ignatius mentions Paul's conversion on the road to Damascus and Matthew's immediate decision to become a disciple when Jesus called him. This sudden, lightning-bolt flash from heaven happens less often than some people think. A jubilant announcement that "God told me to do this" might be a false consolation from **the evil spirit** that needs to be carefully examined. (See **Rules for the Discernment**

of Spirits.) But no-doubt-about-it decisions do happen. God can intervene directly if he wants to, and sometimes he does.

When our feelings are engaged.

Often we feel conflicting emotions when we have to decide something important—confusion, excitement, fearfulness, hope, anxiety, or a desire to see the whole matter go away. Here the way forward lies in observing and interpreting these feelings. This is the classic case of Ignatian discernment. Our hearts are divided. Part of us wants to draw closer to God and part of us wants our own way. This struggle generates feelings of **consolation and desolation**; properly interpreted, these feelings point to the choice that will best serve God and give us the greatest joy. This is how Ignatius himself came to conversion to Christ. He realized that the peace and joy that he felt when imagining a life as Jesus' disciple was a sure sign that this was a choice he should make.

Although he doesn't say so directly, Ignatius probably thought that this is the best way to make decisions. He believed that our hearts give us a sounder and deeper understanding of God than our minds do.

When we're not feeling much of anything.

Sometimes, though, strong feelings are not present. We look at two alternatives and feel no enthusiasm one way or another, and no aversion to either. God isn't saying anything. Nothing much is happening in prayer. It's a muddle. Ignatius offers two approaches to a decision in these circumstances.

The first approach is to tackle the problem analytically. Make a list of the pros and cons of each choice, pray over them, ask God to direct your heart to the right choice. Eventually the right choice will become clear.

The second approach employs the imagination. Ignatius suggests several clever scenarios to help you think differently about the options in front of you, and most likely to get your feelings involved too.

Scenario one: Imagine that you are meeting with someone who is struggling with the very same decision you are facing. This person, whom you've never met before, describes the situation to you. You listen to the story. What do you feel as you listen? What seems important? What seems less relevant? The person asks you for advice. You think about it a bit, and then you speak. What do you say? This exercise can help you achieve some detachment from your situation and see it objectively.

Scenario two: Imagine that you're on your deathbed, and you are looking back on the time when you made this decision. What choice do you wish you had made? This can help you look at the long-term consequences of your decision, and guard against putting too much emphasis on an immediate benefit.

Scenario three: Imagine that you are standing before God at the Last Judgment. In this spot, which choice do you wish you had made? This can help clarify the moral implications of your decision.

No matter how a decision is made, it needs to be confirmed. Ignatius is insistent on this point. Often this step is neglected or skipped entirely. A tentative decision can morph into a final one without your noticing it. Ignatius says we should turn "with great diligence to prayer" and ask God to confirm the decision.

Desire

My friend Ben, a Jesuit priest, drove out of a parking structure one afternoon. He stopped at the cashier's booth and handed his ticket to the man sitting inside. The cashier, who looked to be in his thirties, had a mournful air about him. He took a long look at Ben, who was wearing his Roman collar that day, and said, "Father, my life is meaningless. What shall I do?"

Ben thought the man might be asking a serious question. He glanced in his mirror at the cars lined up behind him. He had a couple of seconds to say something useful. He replied, "Think about the things you most desire and talk to God about them."

Ben's answer came straight out of the Ignatian tradition. Ignatius loved desires. He believed that desire is the main way we discover who we are and what we are meant to do. That's how Ignatius himself found his way. Desire, for him, was the key to a fulfilling life. In *my* tradition—the mid-century Irish Catholic subculture I grew up in—desire meant trouble. It meant sexual desire and the longing for wealth, power, glory, and fame that good people were supposed to resist. There's some truth to that, but Ignatius believed that our deepest desires are to love and serve God and other people. God has given us these desires; so, when we know what they are, we know what God wants. That's why Ignatius constantly urges us to get in touch with our desires. Many times in the Spiritual Exercises, Ignatius says "pray for what you want." Talk to God about it.

William A. Barry, SJ points out that we're often encouraged in subtle ways to neglect or suppress our desires. When we want something, we're told to be grateful for what we already have. When we're miserable, we're told to suck it up because the experience is good for us. "But if we suppress our desires without being satisfied that God has heard us, we pull back from honesty with God," Barry says. "We need to keep letting God know our real desires until we are satisfied or have heard or felt some response."

So when you go on an Ignatian retreat or talk to an Ignatian spiritual director, expect to hear about desires. Consider what you most desire and talk to God about it.

Discernment

If a genie appeared from a magic lamp and promised to grant me one wish, I'd ask for perfect skill in discernment. What could be more valuable than the ability to determine the right thing to do? Discernment is the ability to separate what's important from what's irrelevant or misleading. It's a great skill for the problems of everyday life: how to tackle the "to do" list, how to love the people we love, how to love the people who drive us nuts. Discernment is needed even more for the bigger life questions around career, vocation, commitments, and duty.

In the Ignatian tradition, discernment is both a skill and a methodology. The skill is learning how to interpret spiritual senses and inner movements of the heart. The methodology is applying these skills (and other tools) to the choices we face in real life.

The best way to explain Ignatian discernment is to tell the story of Ignatius's conversion. At its core, it's a drama of discernment. The young Ignatius was trained as a soldier in service to the Kingdom of Navarre. In 1521, he was badly wounded defending the city of Pamplona from an assault by the French army. (The French were much stronger, and Ignatius would have been wiser to surrender. The city fell shortly after he did.) Ignatius was carried home to the family castle in the town of Loyola, where he endured two surgeries to repair shattered legs. He faced many months of recovery. To pass the time, he read the only books in the house—a life of the saints and a life of Christ. Ignatius had an active imagination. Sometimes he would daydream about his past exploits as a courtier, ladies' man, and warrior; then he would daydream about living like Christ and the saints.

Eventually he noticed something: his **feelings** didn't match the content of his reveries. As he wrote in his *Autobiography*:

> There was this difference. When he was thinking of those things of the world, he took such delight in them, but afterwards, when he was tired and put them aside, he found himself dry and dissatisfied. But when he thought of going to Jerusalem barefoot, and of eating

nothing but plain vegetables and of practicing all the other rigors that he saw in the saints, not only was he consoled when he had these thoughts, but even after putting them aside he remained satisfied and joyful.

Fantasies of the fun life left him feeling sad; thoughts of a hard life left him feeling happy. A puzzlement, but it's a pretty common experience. You have a big date, a night out with the guys—and you feel glum and depressed afterwards. You visit a sick friend, tackle a project that you've been dreading—and you feel pretty good, as if your best self came out of hiding. Ignatius realized that the spirits were working in these feelings—the Holy Spirit and **the evil spirit**. God was trying to tell him something. His fantasies represented two directions his life could take, and God was using his feelings about them to point him in the right direction. The joy he felt when he imagined being a disciple of Christ meant that this life would bring him greatest satisfaction.

The main elements of Ignatian **discernment** are all here. Ignatius achieved the skill of reflective **awareness** of the shifting inner moods and feelings. He recognized the states of **consolation and desolation** and understood that they were produced by spiritual forces. Central to the whole experience was **desire**; his deepest yearning was to be a disciple of Christ, and discernment led him to realize that.

Ignatius said that "his eyes were opened a little" by this insight. He learned much more as time went on. He saw that the states of consolation and desolation arise from ceaseless spiritual conflict in our divided hearts. We want God, but we want many things other than God: fame, money, power, our own way. Ignatius called these **disordered affections**. To a great degree, discernment involves identifying these attachments and separating ourselves from them so that they don't govern us. The goal is freedom—what Ignatius called **indifference**—not pulled this way or that, free to choose the course that gives greater glory to God.

Ignatius summarized his understanding of discernment in twenty-two **rules for the discernment of spirits**, which he appended to the Spiritual Exercises. They are organized into two sets. The first set shows how to cope with the experiences of desolation; the second set mainly concerns the problem of false consolation—the fact that the evil spirit can mislead us by manipulating feelings of consolation.

In the practice of Ignatian discernment, we ask this question: Is this action consistent with who I am and who I want to become? We can answer this question with confidence if we sincerely love God and seek to follow in the footsteps of Christ.

Disordered Affections

The hard work of **discernment** comes in overcoming disordered affections, or disordered attachments, as Ignatius sometimes called them. These are the things that we are in love with. They are *affections*; we love them, nurture them, keep them safe. They are also *attachments*; they limit our freedom. They are the things we *must* have. Author Chris Lowney calls this problem the "I-want-it-so-badly virus." He writes:

> I so wanted to get to the top of the company, or to attract that attractive person, or to be rich, or to be recognized as important, or to have the best house, or to have a more exciting life. In fact, we sometimes delude ourselves into thinking that the object of our affection (the job, the car, the partner, the house) must be right for us precisely because we want it so badly.

Confronting disordered affections can be uncomfortable—almost any **desire** can become a disordered attachment: a desire to make money, a yearning to be admired, a determination to give the orders instead of following them, physical fitness, sexual pleasure, having cool friends. All these things, and many others, can become the ends we pursue. They are disordered—literally out of order. They crowd out everything else. There's nothing wrong with making money, but there's probably a lot wrong if you work all the time. There's nothing wrong with enjoying admiration and praise, but something's out of whack if your craving for the limelight distorts your judgment.

Discerning when affections become disordered is difficult. We usually don't want to look too closely at the things that drive us. Usually motives are mixed. The motives for any important decision typically include the practical and the idealistic, the selfish and the generous, the fearful and the trusting, the realistic and the fanciful. Do we have too little ambition or too much? Are we too passive or too aggressive? What's "enough" money?

The goal is to reach what Ignatius called **indifference**—that point of freedom and detachment where we can make the choices that satisfy our deepest desires. Indifference means that disordered attachments no longer have a hold on us. We may still need to take them into account. We might even still love them. But we're not controlled by them. We're open to what God wants, which is what we most deeply want as well.

The Evil Spirit

Central to the Ignatian outlook is the conviction that we live in a condition of perpetual spiritual conflict. Ignatius had many words for the malevolent spiritual entity that seeks to turn us away from God—the "bad spirit," "bad angel," and "Lucifer" appear frequently in his writings, but his favorite is "enemy." He calls it "the enemy," "our enemy," "the enemy of our progress and eternal salvation," and often, "the enemy of our human nature." We face serious, sustained opposition on our journey to God, and it's personal. Lucifer is *our* enemy.

Ignatius depicts our enemy as a malign intelligence who operates through deceit. This isn't the monstrous devil—almost as powerful as God—that children are taught to fear. He's a cunning, patient, and resourceful spirit, adept at distortion and treacherous implication. To overcome this enemy, we need to expose his lies. That's why Ignatian spirituality emphasizes self-knowledge and the danger of being misled. One of Ignatius's most perceptive comments is a remark in one of the **rules for the discernment of spirits,** that bad ideas and disastrous mistakes present themselves in attractive garb:

> It is a mark of the evil spirit to assume the appearance of an angel of light. He begins by suggesting thoughts that are suited to a devout soul, and ends by suggesting his own. For example, *he will suggest holy and pious thoughts* that are wholly in conformity with the sanctity of the soul [emphasis added]. Afterwards, he will endeavor little by little to end by drawing the soul into his hidden snares and evil designs.

It's bad enough when greed or pride or lust lead us into poor choices; it's downright scary to think that "holy and pious thoughts" can lead us astray too. That's why we need **discernment**. Some people think that discernment is finished when they're feeling good about what they think God wants them to do. Ignatius says that this is where discernment begins. We need to prayerfully examine *everything*—even, and most especially, our yearning for holiness, community, and service to others.

Do we have to take this talk of evil spirits literally in the twenty-first century? Couldn't this be old-fashioned language for misfortunes that we now know are caused by mental illness and unjust social structures? It's hard to see how medicine and economics can explain the evil in the world. As one theologian put it, "I can understand people who do not believe in God, but the fact that there are people who don't believe in the devil is beyond my comprehension."

Examen

The Daily Examen has been the gateway into Ignatian spirituality for many people. It was for me. I started on the Ignatian path when I learned about this method of prayer that helped me find God in the activities of my daily life. It is simple, practical, and down to earth. There are many versions of the Examen, but the form used most often is based on one that Ignatius offers at the beginning of the Spiritual Exercises.

1. Give thanks.

Look at your day in a spirit of gratitude. Everything is a gift from God.

2. Pray for light.

Begin by asking God for the grace to pray, to see, and to understand.

3. Review the day.

Guided by the Holy Spirit, look back on your day. Pay attention to your experience. Look for God in it.

4. Look at what's wrong.

Face up to failures and shortcomings. Ask forgiveness for your faults. Ask God to show you ways to improve.

5. Make a resolution for the day to come.

What will you do today? Where do you need God today?

The first step is **gratitude**—to consciously adopt an outlook of thanksgiving for the blessings of our lives. This isn't putting on a pair of rose-colored glasses; it's a recognition of the deepest truth—that we are blessed by a loving God who is generous beyond our imagining. The second step is to pray for enlightenment to see our lives through God's eyes; we want the Holy Spirit to show us what we cannot see ourselves.

The heart of the Examen is the third step—a review of the previous day. It's a prayer of memory. Ignatius suggests going through the day in sequence "one hour after another"—the places you've been, the people you've encountered, the work you did. Think of it as watching a home movie of your day. As you watch, note the **feelings** that arise. Strong feelings—positive and negative—usually point to something of importance. Let them surface, look at them, ask the Holy Spirit to show you what they are saying about God's presence in your life and your response to it.

It's hard to tell in advance what will turn out to be significant in your Examen. Dennis Hamm, SJ, calls the Examen "rummaging for God." Everyone has a junk drawer around the house—a drawer full of stuff—pens and pencils, keys, notepaper, business cards, receipts, small tools, and mysterious odds and ends. The drawer is everything that happened in the previous twenty-four hours. In the Examen you're rummaging around in it, looking for the couple of things that are especially significant.

The fourth step is to recognize and correct what went wrong in the day just past. The fifth and final step is to resolve to act in love in the day ahead.

People like the Examen because it anchors our connection to God in our everyday human experience. God is *here*, not *up there*. He's present in our lives, and we can find him there. The Examen helps us with the question, "What do I pray about?" The answer: everything that's happened in the last twenty-four hours. We can find God in all of it—in every task, every encounter, every happening.

For Ignatius, the Examen was literally indispensable. He realized that busy Jesuits, caught up in the demands of an active ministry, might not have time to pray in the usual ways. But he insisted that they always pray the Examen twice a day—at noon and at the end of the day.

People who make a habit of praying the Examen usually do it at the end of the day; it takes about fifteen minutes. But an Examen can be done anywhere—stuck in traffic, eating lunch, walking to class, standing in line, even in meetings. It becomes a habit; you begin to think reflectively, looking for the spiritual movements that are always present in the flow of daily life. I think that is the real purpose of the Examen—to make us **contemplatives in action**, sensitive to the presence of God at *all* times, not just during moments of prayer.

Faber, Peter, SJ

Neurotics throughout the world cheered in 2013 when **Pope Francis** made one of their own a saint. He is Peter Faber (also known as Pierre Favre), one of the founders of the Jesuits. If the church ever wanted to name a patron saint for self-loathing depressives, Faber would be a good choice. His story is a drama of personal transformation. Faber overcame serious personal problems to become a joyful and zealous servant of God.

Faber was born in 1506 in a tiny village in the French Alps called Villaret. His parents were peasants; as a boy he worked as a shepherd. He was very smart, something the local parish priest noticed, and he received an education. Eventually he landed at the University of Paris, where he began studying for an advanced degree. Peter arrived in Paris with a load of personal baggage that would doubtless be recognized today as neurotic traits. He was brooding and introspective. His spiritual life was crippled by scrupulosity. He was indecisive, uncertain about his future, and prone to bouts of depression.

When it came to college roommates, Peter hit the jackpot; he moved into a boarding house with Ignatius Loyola and **Francis Xavier**. Ignatius introduced him to a loving God who pours out gifts of grace, and he explained the dynamics of the spiritual life. He taught Peter how to hear and respond to Christ's invitation to live a life of love and service.

Ignatius's counsel and the experience of the Exercises made Faber a new man. The unsure, scrupulous depressive became a cherished friend and a cheerful, confident servant of Christ. "Always serve Christ the Lord with gladness," he wrote. "Jesus can never be taken from us." His pessimistic view of life was transformed and became expansive and optimistic: "Everywhere there is good to be done, everywhere there is something to be planted and harvested. For we are indebted to all men in every condition and in every place."

Peter was one of the seven **companions** who founded the Jesuits. The pope and his Jesuit superiors sent him all over Europe to promote reform of the church. He worked with university students, gave the Spiritual Exercises to hundreds if not thousands of people, built up the new Jesuit order, and made friends everywhere he went.

I especially admire Peter for his great love. At a time when Europe was convulsed by religious hatred, he insisted that Catholics must love Protestants: "We must be careful to have great charity for them and love them in truth, banishing from the soul all considerations that would tend to chill our esteem for them. We need to win their goodwill, so that they will love us and accord us a good place in their hearts." He's talking about genuine esteem and love, not good manners. You can't fake this. It's possible only if we allow God's mercy to change our hearts.

"Take care never to close your heart to anyone," he said.

Feelings

Feelings were of primary importance to Ignatius. He thought that our hearts bring us closer to God than our minds do. He told directors of the Spiritual Exercises to be very concerned if the people they are guiding weren't feeling anything. Without feelings, the Exercises will grind to a halt.

Ignatian spirituality is concerned with feelings in the broadest sense; they include the whole range of moods, emotions, leadings, intuitions, and senses that constitute the affective part of our minds. Psychologists talk about the three parts of the mind: the *cognitive* (reason and other mental processes), the *conative* (the will), and the *affective* (feelings and emotions). All are important, but the engine that drives the train is the affective power. The traditional term for it is "the heart"—our inner orientation, the core of our being, the things we love. This is what Jesus referred to when he told us to store up treasures in heaven instead of on earth, "for where your treasure is, there your heart will be also" (Luke 12:34). The heart is what Ignatius was after. The key to it, he thought, lies in those deep currents of feeling that shape what we want, which in turn influence what we do.

Paying close attention to emotions and moods has never been easy. **Peter Faber** complained about pious retreatants who lived in their heads. He wanted them to get in touch with the Holy Spirit, which, he said, "appears through desires, motions, ardor or despondency, tranquility or anxiety, joy or sorrow, and other analogous spiritual motions." The message is clear: when you enter the world of Ignatian **discernment** and **spiritual direction**, be ready to dwell on your feelings.

Finding God in All Things

On occasion I've had to describe Ignatian spirituality very quickly to someone who knows nothing about it. I'll be at a party or at a neighborhood picnic, and someone I don't know will ask me what I'm writing about. I'll say, "Ignatian spirituality—the spirituality of the Jesuits" (everybody's heard of the Jesuits). And then I'll add, "It's a spirituality that finds God in all things."

The early Jesuits used the phrase to describe their spirituality. Ignatius often said that "we must find God in all things," according to **Jerome Nadal**, his closest collaborator. He said of Ignatius: "In all things, actions, conversations, he felt and contemplated the presence of God." For Ignatius, this was not a vague sentiment, but a real program of prayer. In a letter to the superior of a group of young Jesuits in training, he said that the men shouldn't spend too much time in formal prayer because they had other work to do.

Instead, "They should practice the seeking of God's presence in all things, in their conversations, their walks, in all that they see, taste, hear, understand, in all their actions, since His Divine Majesty is truly in all things." He added that this way of praying is "easier than raising oneself to the consideration of divine truths which are more abstract." Amen to that.

The idea of finding God in all things is rooted in the **Contemplation to Attain the Love of God** at the end of the **Spiritual Exercises**. God is described as a being who dwells in all things, who works and labors to renew his creation, and who showers us with an endless stream of blessings and gifts like the sun bathes the earth in light and warmth. This generous God is radically *here* in the created world, in human culture, and the everyday world of our personal experience. He is truly present in all things.

This explains why you find Jesuits programming computers, making art, digging wells, studying the stars, baking bread, and generally busying themselves in every nook and cranny of human learning and culture. It explains the liberality and expansiveness of the Ignatian outlook: If God is present in all things, then nothing can be excluded from the spiritual life; frustration and sorrow are as much a part of it as peace and joy. The spiritual life can take place at any time and in any place, not just in special places like a church. Finding God in all things also explains the restlessness and dynamism of Ignatian spirituality. "All things" never ends; there will always be more to learn about God, some new thing will always come along to reveal God in fresh and surprising ways.

Fourth Vow

A big part of the Jesuit mystique is the so-called fourth vow of special obedience to the pope. All professed members of Catholic religious orders make vows of poverty, chastity, and obedience. Jesuits add a fourth promise of "special obedience to the sovereign pontiff with regard to missions." That's why Jesuits became known as the "pope's army" during the Counter-Reformation. They were an elite, educated force filled with missionary **zeal** sworn to go where the pontiff sent them in mission.

The fourth vow has been widely misunderstood, sometimes by the Jesuits themselves. First of all, it is a promise to obey the pope *with regard to missions*—that is, in matters affecting the mission of the Society of Jesus to "help souls." For Ignatius and his **companions**, the vow was a way to obtain a broad, universal perspective on their work without being biased by their own nationalities and ethnicities.

They wanted to go where the need was greatest; they presumed that the pope, as the leader of the universal church, was in the best position to determine this. The fourth vow is not a promise to do anything the pope wants; Ignatius himself was frequently displeased with papal actions, and he sometimes opposed them.

The fourth vow does not mean that the pope is able to order Jesuits around. Early on it was understood that the fourth vow also applied to the **Superior General** of the Jesuits, who also had a broad perspective. As a practical matter, Jesuits receive their assignments from their superiors in the ordinary way, just like the members of other religious orders.

Still, the Jesuits' special connection to the papacy has been a thorny issue for centuries. It entangled the Jesuits in secular political controversies because the pope was the temporal ruler of the papal states, and he was frequently at odds with France, Spain, and other countries. Jesuits in these countries, loyal to the pope, were accused of helping the nation's enemies. Jesuits often invoked papal protection when their methods and work angered powerful secular and church authorities. And, because many Jesuits interpreted the fourth vow to mean that they must defend the papacy no matter what the issue, they made enemies.

All this contributed to the **suppression of the Jesuits** in 1773, the greatest disaster in the Society's history. One of the many reasons for it was the Jesuits' fierce defense of the papacy at a time when the leading states of Europe were struggling to assert their independence from Rome. After the order was restored in 1814, the Society doubled down on the papal connection. Throughout the nineteenth century, most Jesuits stood with the papacy in its opposition to liberalizing social, political, and intellectual movements. They supported the popes' efforts to centralize church authority, and they helped Pope Pius IX define the dogma of papal infallibility at the First Vatican Council.

In the twentieth century, the pendulum swung in the other direction. Jesuits no longer rushed to defend the pope against all criticism, and they more readily supported movements of church and social reform. Some Jesuits openly opposed the hierarchy, and some Jesuits advanced highly controversial theological views that angered church officials. In the minds of some powerful prelates, a cloud of suspicion surrounded the Society. This came to a head in 1981 when Pope John Paul II appointed his own personal delegate to run the Society when **Pedro Arrupe**, the Superior General, became incapacitated. After a couple of years, normal governance was restored and the Jesuits elected a new Superior

General. The election of the first Jesuit pope in 2013 is a hopeful sign that feelings of mistrust have dissipated.

Friendship with God

One of the most appealing Ignatian ideas is the notion that we can relate to God like a friend. Ignatius says as much: "I talk with Jesus like a friend," he writes in the Spiritual Exercises. He urges us to talk to Jesus "as one friend to another, making known his affairs to him and seeking advice in them." The Jesuit spiritual writer **William A. Barry**, SJ, says that friendship is always on God's mind. "God desires humans into existence for the sake of friendship," he writes in his book *A Friendship Like No Other*.

Of course, Ignatius and his companions didn't invent the idea that a relationship with God can be intimate. The Bible is full of images of God's tender mercy and love for us, and Jesus calls his disciples "friends." There's a rich Christian tradition of devotion and prayer that's meant to bring God close. And there is another devotional tradition that emphasizes God's majesty and apartness, and counts the "fear of the Lord" among the great virtues. These traditions wax and wane in the life in the church.

The Ignatian tradition is to hold God close. The dynamic of the Spiritual Exercises is to get to know **Jesus** intimately as a friend, companion, and mentor. We walk with him and strive to think and act like him. Ignatius thought that once Jesus becomes your friend, everything else will fall into place.

Intimacy with Jesus is one of the themes of **Pope Francis**'s preaching. An example: "Let the risen Jesus enter your life—welcome him as a friend, with trust: he is life! If up till now you have kept him at a distance, step forward. He will receive you with open arms." Words like these come straight from the pope's **Jesuit formation**.

Generosity, Prayer for

Ignatius's prayer for generosity is one of my favorites.

> Lord, teach me to be generous,
> to serve you as you deserve,
> to give and not to count the cost,
> to fight and not to heed the wounds,
> to toil and not to seek for rest,
> to labor and not to look for any reward,
> save that of knowing that I do your holy will.

The problem is that Ignatius had nothing to do with this prayer. Not even close. The oldest publication of it dates from 1910, where it appeared as "The Scout's Prayer" in a French Boy Scout manual. Jesuits were active in the French Scout movement at the time, and one of them may have written it. The famous Prayer of St. Francis ("Lord, make me an instrument of your peace . . . ") has a similar unexpected history. It was written in 1912 by a writer for a

French Catholic magazine, more than seven centuries after Francis's death.

Disappointing? Not really. I think it's great that a modern prayer can capture the spirit of a saint so well that people think the saint wrote it. In Ignatius's case, the Prayer for Generosity expresses wholehearted commitment, a desire to imitate Christ, a generous spirit, and a readiness to work hard—all sentiments associated with Ignatian spirituality and the Spiritual Exercises. They fit Ignatius perfectly. It feels as if he could have written that prayer, just as St. Francis could have written the prayer attributed to him. It shows how robust these spiritual traditions are that centuries later they produce prayers that sound just like the founders.

God's Will

During my checkered youth I ran into some evangelical Protestants who swore by something they called "The Four Spiritual Laws." The first law, "God loves you and has a wonderful plan for your life," is a version of a pretty common idea: that God's will is something external to us, a blueprint that we have to follow. This model has logical problems. How detailed is the blueprint? Does God have a plan for every detail of our lives? Where does God's plan end and our free choice begin? Another problem is that the blueprint model makes doing God's will a power relationship: God is all-powerful and he has all the answers. We need to comply.

In the Spiritual Exercises, doing God's will is a matter of love and **desire**. Ignatius's view of it is summed up in a meditation note: "To behold myself standing in the presence of God our Lord and of all His saints, that I may know and desire what is more pleasing to His Divine Goodness." Doing God's will occurs within a loving relationship. There's a mutuality about it. God deeply desires something to be done; we deeply desire to know what it is so we can do it. It's something we do together. This partnership is a consequence of the astounding miracle of the **Incarnation**: by becoming human, God agreed to accomplish his purposes through the free choices of human beings.

Ignatius says that God can be found in all things; there's no blueprint, no spec sheet, no user's manual. God does not have one right answer for us. The good is plural. God is abundant, not limiting. Most of our choices are among the good, better, and best—not right and wrong. In the Ignatian perspective, "God's will" isn't something external. It's implanted in our hearts. Doing God's will is more a matter of growing into the kind of person we're meant to be. The question to ask is: Is this action consistent with who I am and who I want to become? To put it another way, the question is: *What do I really want?* When we know what we really want, we know what God wants.

Gratitude

Ignatius's friends remembered him as a man overflowing with gratitude. Diego Laínez, one of the first **companions**, recalled:

> . . . . at night Ignatius would go up on the roof of the house, with the sky there up above him. He would sit quietly, absolutely quietly. He would take his hat off and look up for a long time at the sky. Then he would fall to his knees, bowing profoundly to God. . . . And the tears would begin to flow down his cheeks like a stream, but so quietly and gently that you heard not a sob or a sigh nor the least possible movement of his body.

For Ignatius, our relationship with God is founded on gratitude. God is the infinitely generous giver of gifts and blessings; we respond with gratitude and profuse thanks. "We will much sooner tire of receiving his gifts than he of giving them," Ignatius wrote to a friend. The first step of the **Examen** is to "give thanks to God our Lord for the favors received." This is the deepest truth about our spiritual condition—that we are in a relationship with a loving God who is generous beyond our wildest dreams.

Gratitude was so important to Ignatius that he believed ingratitude was the deadliest of sins. Out of all evils, he wrote, "Ingratitude is one of the things most worthy of detestation." So much so, he continued, that ingratitude is "the cause, beginning, and origin of all evils and sins." This remark startled me when I ran across it. I thought that pride is the deadliest of the seven deadly sins. But where does pride come from? Ignatius suggests that it's rooted in that sense that we are entitled to the good things we have, or that we've somehow acquired them through our own efforts. In other words, pride stems from ingratitude.

Toward the end of the Spiritual Exercises, Ignatius urges us to pray for gratitude: "To ask for an intimate knowledge of the many blessings received, that filled with gratitude for all, I may in all things love and serve the Divine Majesty."

Helping Souls

The Jesuits have two mottos. The better-known one is ***Ad majorem Dei gloriam*** ("For the greater glory of God"). But the early Jesuits more often used another phrase to describe their purpose: "helping souls." The Jesuit **Constitutions** say "our vocation is to travel through the world and to live in any part of it where there is hope of greater service to God and of help of souls."

"Helping souls" expresses the heart of Ignatian spirituality. It's a spirituality of active service, of helping others in their spiritual and material well-being. The heart of the experience of the **Spiritual Exercises** is meditating on the Gospel accounts of Jesus in action. The purpose of the Exercises is to form us as disciples who will do the work of love in the circumstances we find ourselves in. "The decision to follow Christ is to follow him as humble, poor, and rejected within a culture that values wealth, power, influence, and prestige," says the spiritual director Howard Gray, SJ. "The Exercises are relentlessly oriented toward the life one lives outside of solitude—in the arena of public life, to the future."

"Helping souls" can be risky. A Jesuit once wrote to Ignatius saying he feared for the safety of his soul if he worked at the court of the King of Portugal, a notorious cesspool of corruption and skullduggery. Ignatius admonished him: "Your personal safety is not relevant," he said. "If we were supposed to subordinate the good we do to keeping clear of danger, then we would not have to live among people and have contact with them. But according to our vocation we have contact with everyone." Point made, but Ignatius reassured him: "If we go about with our intention upright and pure, then Christ himself will look after us in his infinite goodness."

Hopkins, Gerard Manley, SJ

The British Jesuits at Campion Hall at Oxford introduced me to the poetry of Gerard Manley Hopkins when I lived there during my junior year abroad. Hopkins was one of their own; he's probably the most famous British Jesuit, regarded as one of the greatest poets in the English language. His verse is full of gorgeous language, extravagant imagery, and deep feeling. I took to it immediately.

Ironically, Hopkins's Jesuit career was sad and dreary. His health was poor, and he was plagued by bouts of severe depression. He did not distinguish himself in parish ministry or in teaching in Jesuit schools in England and Ireland. He died of typhoid fever at the age of forty-four. He kept his poetry to himself. He showed his poems to only a few close friends, and they weren't published until after his death.

Much of Hopkins's poetry deals with spiritual desolation. But the one that you will see quoted all the time in Ignatian circles (and beyond) is "God's Grandeur," about **finding God in all things**.

> The world is charged with the grandeur of God.
>   It will flame out, like shining from shook foil;
>   It gathers to a greatness, like the ooze of oil
> Crushed. Why do men then now not reck
>   his rod?
> Generations have trod, have trod, have trod;
>   And all is seared with trade; bleared, smeared
>   with toil;
>   And wears man's smudge and shares man's
>   smell: the soil
> Is bare now, nor can foot feel, being shod.
> And for all this, nature is never spent;
>   There lives the dearest freshness deep down
>   things;
> And though the last lights off the black
>   West went
>   Oh, morning, at the brown brink eastward,
>   springs—
> Because the Holy Ghost over the bent
>   World broods with warm breast and with ah!
>   bright wings.

Ignatius Loyola

The portrait of Ignatius Loyola that you see most often shows him in middle age, dressed in somber black, with penetrating eyes, a stern expression, and a high forehead suggesting a great intellect. It's a picture of a Great Man, as indeed he was—the founder of the Jesuits, author of the **Spiritual Exercises**, and a towering figure in religious and secular history. But there are other ways to imagine Ignatius, and that's what I want to do here to briefly tell his story. Ignatius was a man of many images.

The Hidalgo. He was born in 1491 into a noble family in the Basque region of what is now northern Spain. His given name was Iñigo; he was the youngest of thirteen children. Iñigo was a hidalgo, a nobleman without a hereditary title and usually without much property. He had high status but meager means—all hat and no cattle, as they say in Texas. He had to make his own way in the world. At the age of thirteen he was sent to the royal court of the kingdom of Castile to serve his father's friend, King Ferdinand's chief treasurer.

Iñigo loved the pageantry and intrigue of the royal court. Here's a contemporary description of the future saint: "He is in the habit of going round in cuirass and coat of mail, wears his hair long to the shoulder, and walks about in a two-colored, slashed doublet with a bright cap." Ignatius's own judgment, delivered years later, is more severe: "He was a man given over to the vanities of the world; with a great and vain desire to win fame, he delighted especially in the exercise of arms." He added the tantalizing detail that he was "fairly free in the love of women." He had a temper. Once he was arrested for brawling in the street, making him one of the few saints with a police record.

But Iñigo wasn't just a hot-headed party boy. He was trained as an administrator, and he did good work for the royal treasurer, his patron. He was said to be a man of "great ingenuity and prudence in worldly affairs and very skillful in the handling of men, especially in composing difficulties and discord." When his patron died in 1517, he quickly found another job.

The Soldier. Iñigo became the right-hand man for the viceroy of Navarre. When war came, he put on his armor, took up a sword, and learned the art of soldiering. Iñigo loved it. With his passion to win fame and glory, and his skill in leading men, he was well suited to lead others in the brutal combat of late medieval warfare. In May 1521, a large French army invaded northern Spain and threatened the city of Pamplona. Iñigo led the defense of the city, but late in the day an artillery ball hit him, shattering his right leg and injuring the other. The city fell, and the victorious French, with great chivalry, treated his wounds and carried him back to his home to recover.

Iñigo endured two horrific surgeries without anesthetics to repair his legs. When he fell gravely ill with a fever, a priest was called to administer the last rites. But his condition gradually improved, and he settled into a long recuperation that lasted a year. He lay on a bed in a room in the family castle in the town of Azpeitia, and was cared for by his sister. He was thirty years old, unmarried, and his military career over because of his injuries. He had ample time to wonder what to do with his life. The room where Ignatius spent that year of recovery, now called the Chapel of Conversion, is a feature on Ignatian pilgrimages. The conversion that happened there is one of the most consequential events in church history.

The Pilgrim. Iñigo's conversion began with his imagination. There were only two books in the Loyola castle—a life of Christ and a life of the saints—and he read and reread them. The stories inflamed his imagination. The stories of the saints excited him, especially the stories of St. Dominic and St. Francis of Assisi. Competitive as ever, he thought he could be an even greater saint if he put his mind to it. He could think of nothing more thrilling than the prospect of giving up everything and following Christ.

But he dreamed about other things too. He imagined that he might return to his former life—he could once again be the swashbuckling young man at the king's court, charming the ladies, impressing his buddies, and gaining in power and influence as he succeeded in the treacherous game of court politics. Over time though, Iñigo realized that his daydreams were affecting him differently. After he dreamed of adventure and glory, he felt sad and discontented. But after he imagined a life imitating the saints and serving Christ, he felt excited and happy. He understood that God was speaking to him through these alternating moods of joy and discontent. He would later label them **consolation and desolation**. They were the signs of the presence of the good spirit and **the evil spirit**, pulling him in different directions. "His eyes were opened a little," he later wrote. This is the core insight that led to the Spiritual Exercises and Ignatian **discernment**.

Iñigo decided to follow Christ, and thus became a pilgrim. Pilgrim is the image of Ignatius that I like best. Ignatius travelled a long way on **pilgrimage**, quite literally. For years he travelled all over Europe, mostly on foot. He travelled spiritually as well—his understanding of how best to serve God in a changing world grew slowly, in fits and starts. Years later, when he wrote his *Autobiography*, "the pilgrim" is what Ignatius called himself—the man on a journey.

His first plan was to do exactly what Jesus did: he would spend his life ministering to people in the Holy Land where Jesus had lived. Throughout his life Ignatius was driven by a longing to be as close to the Master as possible. This is a hallmark of Ignatian spirituality. The core of the Spiritual Exercises is a long series of meditations on the life of Jesus. It's no accident that the religious order he founded is called the **Society of Jesus**.

He set out from home in February 1522 and rode his mule more than three hundred miles to the monastery of Montserrat in Catalonia in eastern Spain. There he gave his fine clothes to a poor man, donned a sackcloth, and left his sword at the shrine of the Black Madonna. His old life was over. He went to the village of Manresa not far away, intending to stay a few days, but he stayed almost a year. Iñigo adopted severe penitential practices—strenuous fasting and the like—but stopped when they did him serious physical and spiritual harm. (He discouraged such practices for the rest of his life, and they are not a feature of Ignatian spirituality today.) It was at Manresa that he wrote the reflections and notes that became the Spiritual Exercises.

In 1523 he finally arrived in Jerusalem, which he hoped would be his permanent home, but the Franciscans who administered the Christian holy places were very unhappy to see him. European noblemen who showed up in Jerusalem were often kidnapped by Muslim warlords and held for ransom—something that put other Christians in danger and caused endless headaches for the Franciscans. They told Iñigo he had to leave. When he objected, they ordered him on pain of excommunication to take the next boat home. He reluctantly complied and returned to Barcelona, where his journey swung in another direction.

The Student. Iñigo wanted to teach others about the Christian faith, but the church wouldn't let him do this without the proper credentials. To get a license to teach, he needed a degree. To go to the university, he needed to learn Latin. So the thirty-two-year-old Ignatius, middle-aged by sixteenth-century standards, went back to school with much younger fellow students to satisfy his language requirement.

After two years, he enrolled at the University of Alcalá, just east of Madrid, to study philosophy and theology. Iñigo was not your conventional student. In his free time he served the poor and gave his Spiritual Exercises to people who were drawn to his friendliness and charisma. These activities attracted the attention of the Spanish Inquisition, which was on the lookout for Illuminati—heretics who claimed that God spoke directly to them. The authorities threw him in jail for forty-two days; in the end they released him, unable to find anything wrong with his teaching. The authorities did forbid him to teach about faith until he had a degree.

Seeking a more liberal atmosphere, Iñigo decamped to the University of Salamanca, but he soon wound up in trouble again. This time it was the Dominican friars who were suspicious of him. They detained him for twenty-two days until an inquisitor eventually cleared him. (This is the historical basis for those **Jesuit jokes** that play on a not-so-friendly rivalry between Jesuits and Dominicans.) After this, Iñigo had had enough of Spain. He walked 700 miles north to study at the University of Paris, the greatest center of learning in Europe.

The Friend. There's a fascinating video on YouTube that shows a couple of hundred young people relaxing on a hillside listening to music on a fine summer day. A guy gets up and begins to dance. People stare at him curiously. You can imagine them thinking: *What a weird guy. What's up with him?* The guy keeps dancing alone for a while, people staring. You start to feel embarrassed for him. Then another guy gets up and joins him. Then a girl. Then a fourth and a fifth and a sixth dancer. Then, after a short while, a rush of dancers. Pretty soon almost everyone on the hillside is rocking and rolling and having a great time. The point of the video is to show how important followers are—especially the first followers. The crucial moment in a movement comes when those first followers risk their reputations and get up to join the leader who has been dancing alone.

That's what happened when Iñigo made friends at the University of Paris. For years he had talked to others about God. He attracted a lot of attention. People liked him, but so far no one had joined him. That changed in Paris. In 1529 he moved into a new boarding house. His **companions** were the gifted future saints **Peter Faber** (also known as Pierre Favre), a brilliant, introspective Frenchman, and **Francis Xavier**, a boisterous, charismatic son of a Basque nobleman. Both men completed the Spiritual

Exercises with Iñigo and were inflamed with a **zeal** to serve Christ. Others joined them one by one: Simão Rodrigues, a Portuguese; and the Spaniards Diego Laínez, Alfonso Salmerón, and Nicolás de Bobadilla.

On August 15, 1534, the Feast of the Assumption of Mary, the seven companions gathered in a chapel on the hill of Montmartre north of Paris and made vows to serve God together. This was the nucleus of what would later become the Jesuit order. Ignatius is routinely called the founder of the Jesuits, but it's also true that the Jesuits were founded by a group of companions who discerned their common direction together.

Around this time, Iñigo dropped his given name and started using Ignatius. He never explained why. He may have thought that Ignatius was easier to say, or he may have been inspired by the second-century bishop Ignatius of Antioch, a theologian and martyr. (Or perhaps he foresaw that, in English, the term "Iñigoan spirituality" would never catch on!)

The new companions spent several years learning how to work together and discerning what their ministry would be. Leaving Paris, their first thought was to go to the Holy Land to minister to Muslims, but warfare between Venice and the Turks prevented ships from sailing there. They preached the gospel, cared for the poor, and ministered in hospitals. In 1537, six of the companions, including Ignatius, were ordained priests in Venice. That fall, they decided to call themselves "the company of Jesus," taking the name of "him whom they had as their head." Realizing that they might never be able to travel to Palestine, the companions decided to go to Rome and place themselves at the disposal of the pope.

Pope Paul III received them warmly and put them to work. Several were assigned to teach in Roman universities. The company took over the Church of Santa Maria della Strada, which became the center for what Ignatius called "works of piety"—homes for orphans, prostitutes, Jewish converts, and the poor. On September 27, 1540, Pope Paul formally established the Society of Jesus. According to a "formula" written by Ignatius, it would be "a community founded chiefly to strive for the progress of souls in Christian life and doctrine, and for the propagation of the faith by means of the ministry of the word, the Spiritual Exercises, and works of charity."

The Superior General. On April 8, 1541, the members of the Society elected Ignatius as their first Superior General. The choice was not unanimous; Ignatius was the lone dissenter. He voted for someone else, and he initially declined the position. Perhaps this was an excess of humility; perhaps he genuinely thought that someone else was better suited to lead the Society. There's little doubt that Ignatius did not relish the job. The **Superior General** was elected for life, and Ignatius did not want to spend the rest of his days sitting in an office running a large organization. He wanted to be out in the world, on baptizing missions, preaching to the troubled and disaffected, teaching the ignorant, caring for the sick and the poor, and giving hope to the hopeless.

Instead, he created a religious order that did all these things—and more. Within a few years, Jesuit missionaries were at work in Asia and the Americas. The Jesuits created a network of elite schools educating poor boys as well as the sons of the wealthy—the largest network of schools until the advent of public education in modern times. Jesuit scientists, artists, theologians, and humanists populated the faculties of Europe's elite universities. They gave the Spiritual Exercises and provided **spiritual direction**.

Ignatius shaped a style of ministry that was a sharp departure from the traditional model of religious life. His men were out in the world, often by themselves, not living in a community of monks and friars. He stressed flexibility. He wrote the Society's **Constitutions**, covering governance, training, ministry, and other practical matters. This lengthy document included many exceptions to the rules and exhortations to superiors to be flexible and judicious in applying them. He established high standards for new recruits and insisted that they complete many years of formation. When superiors clamored for more manpower to staff the Society's rapidly growing ministries, Ignatius's response was to tighten admission standards, not relax them. He didn't want frail and faint-hearted men slipping in.

He kept in touch with his far-flung brothers by writing letters—more than 7,000 of them, the largest archive of correspondence of an individual from the sixteenth century. He worked long hours in a small suite of offices in Rome, going to bed late and getting up early. His health, never robust, began to fail in 1556, and he died on July 31 of that year. There were 1,000 Jesuits at the time of his death. When he was canonized in 1622, less than seventy years later, there were 15,000 Jesuits. It was a harvest of astonishing abundance.

Imaginative Prayer

One of the most powerful and distinctive forms of Ignatian prayer is imaginative prayer. Much of the prayer in the **Spiritual Exercises** consists of imaginative contemplation of texts from the Gospels. Spiritual directors often teach this kind of prayer. It is used in **discernment**, and there is an imaginative element to the **Examen**. This way of praying is so identified with Ignatius that it's known in the Christian spiritual tradition as Ignatian contemplation.

Ignatius's imagination played a central role in his conversion. He grasped the work of good and evil spirits by reflecting on the effect his daydreams had on his emotions. He became a disciple of Christ by imagining what it would be like to follow him. He came to know **Jesus** intimately by immersing himself in Gospel stories that showed Jesus healing, teaching, casting out spirits, and walking on the roads of Palestine. He thought that the imagination was an important means of bringing about a conversion, so in the Spiritual Exercises, he wants you to turn your imagination loose.

In the Exercises, Ignatius shows two ways of imagining. The first is to try to see things from God's perspective. A powerful meditation in the second week of the Exercises asks you to imagine the three Persons of the Trinity looking on our turbulent world, full of pain and sorrow, and deciding to save suffering humanity. By imagining the mercy and compassion God felt in bringing about the **Incarnation**, you take on these qualities yourself.

The second method is to experience the gospel from the inside as participants, instead of from the outside as readers. You put yourself within the gospel story and give full rein to your imagination. For example, with the healing of the blind man Bartimaeus (Mark 10:46–52), you imagine yourself standing by the side of the road watching Jesus speak to a blind man, feeling the hot Mediterranean sun, smelling the dust kicked up by the passersby, feeling your itchy clothing, the sweat rolling down your back, the hunger in your belly. You see the blind man's desperation, the disciples' irritation, the curiosity of the onlookers. You pay special attention to Jesus—the way he moves and gestures, the look in his eyes, the expression on his face. You hear him speak the words that are recorded in the Gospel, and you go on to imagine other things he might have said and done.

Ignatius proposes many scenes from the Gospels for imaginative contemplation like this—about fifty of them in all. Most of them are scenes of Jesus doing things, on the move, ministering, interacting with others. Ignatius doesn't want us to *think* about Jesus; he wants us to *experience* him. He wants Jesus to fill your senses. He wants you to *meet* him. Imaginative Ignatian prayer teaches you things about Jesus that you wouldn't learn through Scripture study or theological reflection. It allows the person of Christ to penetrate into places that the intellect does not touch. It brings Jesus into your heart. It engages your **feelings**. It inflames you with ideals of generous service. Imaginative prayer makes the Jesus of the Gospels *your* Jesus.

Imaginative prayer is especially powerful in the third week of the Exercises where the readings take us through Jesus' Passion and death. Ignatius says to pray for the grace of compassion. We are to suffer *with* Jesus. David Fleming, SJ, points out how this teaches us to suffer with the people in our lives.

> When we cannot change a situation, we are tempted to walk away from it. We might literally walk away; we are too busy to sit with a suffering friend. Or we walk

away emotionally; we harden ourselves and maintain an emotional distance. We might react to the gospel accounts of Jesus' passion and death this way. They describe something terrible and horribly painful, yet we might shield ourselves from the pain. We *know* the story of the Passion. Ignatius wants us to *experience* it as something fresh and immediate. We learn to suffer with Jesus, and thus learn to suffer with the people in our lives.

As much as he liked imaginative prayer, Ignatius never said that everyone *must* pray this way. In the Spiritual Exercises, he proposes many ways to pray—with Scripture, the Examen, **conversational** prayer, contemplation. No single method works for everyone; what matters is finding a way to open your heart to God. In fact, Ignatius liked variety in prayer. He once told an intense Jesuit to relax and try some new things, saying, "It is a greater virtue in the soul, and a greater grace, for it to be able to relish its Lord in a variety of duties and in a variety of places, rather than simply in one."

Incarnation

The Incarnation—belief that God in the person of **Jesus** "became flesh and pitched his tent among us"—is the central tenet of Christianity. That puts the Incarnation at the heart of Ignatian spirituality as well. Ignatius wanted people to understand the redemptive love that God has for each of us through the person of Jesus. The goal of the **Spiritual Exercises** is to help us encounter the living, breathing Jesus; become his friend; and live in his company.

Ignatius believed that God is found in the real and the material as well as the spiritual—indeed, we **find God in all things**. As we deepen our **friendship with God**, we become **contemplatives in action**, who embody Christ and make the Word flesh in our daily toil all for the greater glory of God (***ad majorem Dei gloriam***).

Indifference

No Ignatian word causes more consternation than *indifference*. "We must make ourselves indifferent to all created things," Ignatius declares in the **Principle and Foundation**. He goes on: "We should not prefer health to sickness, riches to poverty, honor to dishonor, a long life to a short life. The same holds for all other things." A common reaction to these words is "you've got to be kidding." How can you not care whether you're healthy or sick? Despised or well-liked? But Ignatius means it. Indifference is one of the key planks in the Ignatian platform.

Ignatian indifference isn't apathy or disinterest. By indifference Ignatius means detachment from the hungers and cravings and worries that limit our freedom—things such as craving for fame, worry about what other people think, fears of poverty or loneliness. He called these things **disordered affections**. Though often good in their place, they are "disordered"—out of order—and become a kind of bondage when they dominate our lives and control our decisions. It's no exaggeration to put health and prosperity and reputation on the list of potential disordered affections. They can dominate us as thoroughly as anything.

Indifference is especially useful when we are making important decisions. Joseph Tetlow, SJ, describes the "indifferent" Ignatian mind-set this way:

> We will try not to have made our minds up before we have to, even before the alternatives emerge. We will be alert to having deep-seated prejudices and to making implied or even overt demands on God. . . . We will wait when alternatives are emerging. We will try not to favor one over the other until we are clear whether God is telling us something.

The goal is freedom—"freedom from and freedom for," as Howard Gray, SJ, puts it: "freedom from all created reality and freedom for God's ownership over a person's life."

Jesuit Conspiracy Theories

People with a taste for conspiracy theories have long suspected that the Jesuits are up to no good. Consider the facts: Jesuits are highly disciplined, brilliant men, sworn to obedience, skilled in the rhetorical arts, steeped in spiritual mysteries, founded by an ex-soldier who demanded total commitment, led by a Superior General known as the "black pope." They're everywhere in the world, and you can't spot them because they don't wear traditional religious garb. If you're looking for a shadowy organization behind the unexpected and disturbing events that periodically disrupt the lives of ordinary folk, you're bound to give the Jesuits a hard look.

Jesuits have been blamed for the Spanish Armada, the French Revolution, the sinking of the Titanic, the Holocaust, the Kennedy assassination, and the collapse of world financial markets in 2008. They are said to have a secret military base in North Korea. In 2016, a blogger was confident he'd uncovered a Jesuit plot to nominate a weak candidate named Donald Trump (who attended Fordham University for two years) to assure the election of Hillary Clinton. (Oops.) At a convention of UFO conspiracy theorists in 2011, a researcher argued that the aliens sometimes spotted around UFO sightings were, in fact, creatures created by Jesuits in their secret genetic experimentation labs.

To be fair, the powers that be have sometimes had good reason to be suspicious of the Jesuits. This was especially true in sixteenth- and seventeenth-century England, when Jesuits secretly gave spiritual succor to persecuted Catholics, and Jesuits abroad were supporting regime change. The Founders of the United States were not immune to this British tradition of anti-Jesuitism. In a famous letter, John Adams told Thomas Jefferson,

> I do not like the late resurrection of the Jesuits. . . .
> Shall we not have swarms of them here, in as many
> shapes and disguises as ever a king of the gypsies . . .
> assumed in the shape of printers, editors, writers,
> schoolmasters, etc? . . . If ever any congregation of men
> could merit eternal perdition on earth and in hell, it is
> the Company of Loyola.

In reply, Jefferson tried to calm the excitable Adams. Jesuits will come, he said, but Americans must resist bigotry. "Bigotry is a disease of ignorance, of morbid minds. . . . We are destined to be a barrier against the returns of ignorance and barbarism."

Alas, Jefferson was an optimist; ignorance persists. As long as it does, we'll have Jesuit conspiracy theories.

Jesuit Education

The story goes that a Dominican, a Franciscan, and a Jesuit were walking along, debating the greatness of their orders. Suddenly they had a vision of the Holy Family, with Jesus asleep in a manger and Mary and Joseph looking on in wonderment.

The Franciscan fell to his knees in joy, overcome by the glory of God who came in such humble circumstances.

The Dominican prostrated himself in awe of the staggering miracle of Christ's birth.

The Jesuit sidled up to Joseph, put his arm around his shoulders, and said, "So, have you given any thought to where you will send the boy to school?"

Pick ten strangers off the street and ask them what word comes to mind when you say "Jesuit." Chances are that nine of them will say "schools" or "education." Education has been the primary Jesuit ministry for centuries, and it still is today.

This wasn't Ignatius's original plan. He and his **companions** thought they would be peripatetic missionaries travelling the world, preaching the gospel and helping the needy. He didn't want Jesuits to be stuck in one place, encumbered with property, balancing budgets, and doing all the mundane chores necessary to run institutions. The great model was **Francis Xavier**, a nobleman's son who left Europe on a few days' notice and spent the rest of his life as a missionary in India and Japan. But in 1547, Ignatius agreed to open a school in Messina, Sicily, and education quickly became the Jesuits' principal work.

The Jesuits' timing was right. Europe needed a new system of education in the early sixteenth century. The Protestant Reformation, the printing press, and the rise of Renaissance humanism had broken up the old medieval world, including the old styles of schooling. The voyages of exploration to the Americas and the Orient shook up economic life and changed the way Europeans thought about the world. The Jesuit model of education, which combined the rigor of the medieval university and the innovation of the new humanism, suited the new reality very well.

By the mid-eighteenth century, there were more than 800 Jesuit schools in Europe, Asia, and Latin America. It was an integrated network of humanistic education, the largest system of education ever seen until the advent of modern public schooling.

The **suppression of the Jesuits** in 1773 crippled Jesuit education in Europe. Only a handful of schools reopened after the order was restored in 1814, and the focus of Jesuit education shifted to the Americas and Asia. Of the twenty-eight Jesuit colleges and universities in the United States, twenty-one were founded in the nineteenth century.

Jesuit universities and high schools follow an educational method called the Ignatian Pedagogical Paradigm, a holistic approach to teaching and learning based on the Spiritual Exercises. The core learning elements are Experience, Reflection, and Action. The learner is exposed to educational *experiences*, is guided to *reflect* on and deepen these experiences, and is encouraged to put the new knowledge to work in *action*. This is the core dynamic of the Exercises, which involve reflection on contemplative material with the purpose of making decisions to better serve God. Two other elements are added in the Ignatian Pedagogical Paradigm. *Context* takes into account the learner's cultural background and the society in which learning takes place. *Evaluation* measures the degree to which learning has occurred.

Jesuit secondary schools in the United States want to produce students who are "intellectually competent, open to growth, loving, religious, and committed to promoting justice." These five criteria should be embodied by the graduate of a Jesuit school at graduation, or the "Grad at Grad" for short.

Jesuit Formation

Jesuits spend more time in training than brain surgeons do—about twelve years before ordination and several years after. Ignatius wanted a long formation because Jesuits would be working independently in active ministries in novel, unpredictable circumstances, far away from the watchful eye of superiors, and without the support of a religious community. They had to be fully trained, ready for anything. "The path has many and great difficulties connected with it," Ignatius wrote. Those who enter the Society will have to undergo "long and exacting tests."

The first stage is a two-year stint as a *novice*. Novices make the traditional thirty-day version of the Spiritual Exercises (sometimes called the "Long Retreat") and work in a series of "experiments"—temporary assignments to schools, parishes, social ministries, and other Jesuit works. Some novices are given a hundred dollars or so and told to make a trip across the country—an experiment that puts them in the company of poor people and requires them to rely on the kindness of strangers.

After the novitiate, the Jesuit-in-training becomes a *scholastic* and enters *first studies*—a couple of years studying philosophy and working part-time in active ministry. This is followed by *regency*: two or three years of full-time work in a Jesuit ministry. If this is successful, they move into four years of theological studies at the graduate level. After this (for those entering Holy Orders) comes ordination to the diaconate and, six months to a year later, ordination to the priesthood.

Training doesn't end with ordination. After a couple of years, the Jesuit spends a year of *tertianship*, so named because it's something like a third year of novitiate. The man makes the Long Retreat again, revisits the basics of Ignatian spirituality, and works in ministry, most often with the poor and the ill. He then makes *final vows*—including the **fourth vow** of obedience to the pope in regard to missions. In addition to all this, most Jesuits acquire graduate professional degrees and most do language studies as well. All Jesuits learn English; if English is their first language, they learn Spanish.

Jesuitical

A woman came to her Jesuit friend with a question. "Father," she said, "is it true that Jesuits never give you a straight answer?"

After a moment's reflection he said, "Well, yes and no . . ."

The Jesuits are sometimes accused of being devious, inclined to employ slyly clever reasoning to justify dubious behavior. In the seventeenth century, the French Catholic philosopher Blaise Pascal coined the term *Jesuitical* to describe a style of overly subtle argument that found loopholes in moral laws. The term caught on, especially among the Jesuits' enemies (of which there were many); whether it's a fair criticism is another matter.

That is not to say there isn't a real debate to be had about the role of law in moral **decision making**. In one camp are those who hold that rules protect the integrity of the faith and prevent heresies from creeping in. Here you'll find Pascal and other rigorous, letter-of-the-law moralists. On the other side are those with a more flexible view, who embrace the spirit of the law and value freedom of conscience, stressing the importance of a "case-by-case" approach in moral decisions. The Jesuits are mostly in this camp. Each side is at pains to reconcile divine grace with human freedom. The Ignatian tradition delights in free will and the abundance of grace, sometimes to the dismay of those concerned about protecting the role of God's initiative in salvation. The argument has raged for centuries. It goes on today, and you'll still occasionally hear someone being accused of Jesuitical thinking in the process.

In 2017, the Jesuits moved to reclaim the word *Jesuitical* with the launch of *America* magazine's podcast for young Catholics called "Jesuitical." The editors define this to mean: ". . . . asking the questions no one else is asking. It means bringing the Gospel message to streets, televisions, bars, and anywhere else the issues of the day are being debated. It means paying special attention to the needs of the poor and marginalized in all that we do." Now that's a worthy definition for a Jesuit adjective.

Jesuit Jokes

Jesuit jokes form an entire category of religious humor and typically highlight Jesuit "qualities."

Jesuits are practical. A Franciscan, a Dominican, and a Jesuit were sitting in a room when the lights went out. The Franciscan said, "My brothers, let us take this opportunity to consider the debt we owe to our sister, the light." The Dominican said, "Yes, but let us also take this opportunity to contemplate the difference between light and dark." Meanwhile, the Jesuit went to the basement, found the fuse box, reset the breaker, and turned the lights back on.

Jesuits aren't very pious. A man walked up to a Franciscan and a Jesuit and asked, "How many novenas must you say to get a Mercedes-Benz?" The Franciscan asked, "What's a Mercedes-Benz?" The Jesuit asked, "What's a novena?"

Jesuits take advantage. A Franciscan gets a haircut, then asks how much he owes. The barber says he never charges clergy. The Franciscan thanks the barber and goes home. The next morning, the barber finds a big basket of fresh bread from the Franciscans' kitchens.

An Augustinian gets his hair cut by the same barber. The barber also tells him that he never charges clergy. The next day, the barber receives a nice bottle of wine from the Augustinians' wine cellar.

A Jesuit gets his hair cut, and the barber says that he never charges clergy. The next day, the barber opens his shop to find twelve other Jesuits waiting for him.

Jesuits think they're the best. A Dominican and a Jesuit were debating which order was the greatest. So, they decided to ask for a sign from God. A letter fell down from heaven:

> My sons,
> Please stop bickering about such trivial matters,
> Sincerely,
> God, SJ

Jesuits are devious. A Franciscan and a Jesuit, both smokers, found it difficult to pray for a long time without a cigarette, so they went to their superiors to ask for permission to smoke. When they met, the Franciscan was downcast. "I asked my superior if I could smoke while I pray and he said no." The Jesuit smiled. "I asked my superior if I could pray while I smoke. He said, 'Of course.'"

Jesuits need to be taken down a peg. A mother went to her pastor and explained that her son seemed very interested in becoming a priest. She asked what this would require.

The priest began to explain. "If he wants to become a diocesan priest, he'll have to study for eight years. If he wants to become a Franciscan, he'll have to study for ten years. If he wants to become a Jesuit, he'll have to study for fourteen years."

The mother listened carefully, and as the priest concluded, her eyes brightened. "Sign him up for that last one, Father. He's a little slow!"

Jesuits aren't very holy. A Franciscan dies and goes to heaven, humbly knocks on the door, and is let in without any fanfare. One day, a long time later, he notices lots of commotion. Flowers are arranged, all the candles are lit, and a red carpet is rolled out. He asks an angel what's going on, and is told that they are preparing to welcome a Jesuit into heaven. Perplexed, he asks St. Peter, "Why do you make such a fuss over a Jesuit? You hardly noticed me when I arrived." St. Peter says, "We get Franciscans up here all the time, but this is our first Jesuit in centuries!"

The Jesuits: A Brief History

The date that's most often cited for the founding of the Jesuits is August 25, 1534. On that day, Ignatius Loyola and six friends—including **Francis Xavier** and **Peter Faber**—gathered at a chapel in Montmartre, north of Paris, and made vows to serve God together. This was just a declaration of general intent; it took them years to figure out what that promise meant. So a second date also marks the Jesuits' founding: September 27, 1540. On that day Pope Paul III formally established the **Society of Jesus** as an order in the Catholic Church.

The founding documents gave the Society a broad mandate. Jesuits were to spread the faith and strengthen Christians by preaching and teaching adults, educating children and unlettered persons, sponsoring retreats, and engaging in sacramental ministry. The pope added several other ministries: reconciling the estranged, helping the sick and imprisoned, and performing "any other works of charity, according to what will seem expedient for the glory of God and the common good." This was new. Religious orders had traditionally lived together in communities. Their principal mission had been communal prayer, and their life was ordered by ascetical practices. The Jesuits gave priority to their work in the world. Their long training emphasized deep learning, flexibility, and obedience. Regular penances and long periods of daily prayer were discontinued. The Society was tightly organized and led by a powerful **Superior General**. This form of organization was well suited to seize opportunities as Europeans began to explore the rest of the world and the Modern Era dawned.

The two principal works of the early Jesuits were missions and education. **Francis Xavier** led Jesuit missions to India in 1540, journeyed on to Ceylon, Borneo, Malaysia, and Japan. Jesuits established missions in China, Tibet, Vietnam, the Philippines, French Canada, Mexico, and throughout South America. They took a generally positive view of other religious traditions and strove to express the gospel message in forms familiar to local cultures.

The other great work was education. The Jesuits established a network of schools that melded the Renaissance rediscovery of classical learning with the scholastic structure of Catholic theology and philosophy. By the time of Ignatius's death in 1556, less than two decades after their founding, the Jesuits were operating a network of seventy-four colleges on three continents. Jesuit schools encouraged the study of rhetoric, secular literature, non-European languages, sciences, and the arts. They trained many scholars and public officials, extending the influence of the Society into royal courts and universities. While combatting Protestantism was not an explicit mission of the Society, Jesuit scholars and reformers played an important role in the Counter-Reformation. Their schools strengthened the revival of Catholicism in many European countries.

The Jesuits grew rapidly. By the time of Ignatius's death in 1556, about 1,000 Jesuits were already working throughout Europe and in Asia, Africa, and the New World. By 1626 the number of Jesuits was 15,544, and in 1749 the total was 22,589.

The Jesuits made enemies. They fought with colonial administrators over treatment of indigenous peoples; strict Jansenists accused them of laxity and casuistry; other orders resented their size and influence. Most ominously, the kings of France, Spain, and Portugal thought the Jesuits, loyal to the pope, were a vehicle for papal interference in their affairs. All this led to the **suppression of the Jesuits** in

1773 by Pope Clement XIV, who hoped, mistakenly, that this would mollify his royal enemies. The suppression lasted forty-one years. Pope Pius VII, looking for ways to strengthen the church, restored the order in 1814.

The Jesuits grew rapidly afterwards in numbers and influence. They resumed their missionary work and established many new schools, especially in Asia and the Americas.

In the late twentieth century, the number of Jesuits declined following a trend in the Catholic priesthood and religious orders generally. At the same time, many new Jesuit institutions and organizations were founded, such as the **Cristo Rey Network** of secondary schools in inner cities. Jesuits developed new ministries in ecumenism, communications, and the arts. Under Superior General **Pedro Arrupe,** the Society shifted major resources into work with the poor, refugees, and other disadvantaged people, and established the training of **men and women for others** as the goal of **Jesuit education**. In 2013 Jorge Bergoglio, SJ, became **Pope Francis**, the first Jesuit pope.

In 2015, there were 16,740 Jesuits: 11,986 priests, 2,733 scholastics (students to become priests), 1,268 brothers, and 753 novices. It is the largest religious order in the Catholic Church.

Jesuits I Have Known

The first was Jim Coleman, whom I met a month or so after enrolling at St. Peter's College in Jersey City in 1963. He was a shy, chain-smoking, wickedly funny professor of classics who loved to hang out with the staff of the college newspaper, of which he was in charge. Ralph Dates was a terrific philosophy teacher, and Leo McLaughlin, president of St. Peter's, took a personal interest in me—something that astonished me at the time. The Jesuit who had the biggest impact on me was Joe Landy, a lean, brilliant, acerbic, hyperactive English professor, head of the honors program. He mentored me and sent me to Oxford University for my junior year, where I lived with the Jesuits at Campion Hall.

The Master of Campion Hall was Ted Yarnold, an ecumenist and patristics scholar, who ably ran Campion Hall in tumultuous post-Vatican II times even though he probably would rather have been doing something else. My best friends were Garrett Barden, an Irishman, and Joe Boyle, a Scot, undergraduates like myself, who turned me on to **Gerard Manley Hopkins**'s poetry and gave me the first inklings of the surprising allure of Ignatian spirituality. At Campion Hall I was surrounded by Jesuits who were—how shall I put it—strong personalities? characters? eccentrics? Algy Shearburn was an aging ex-jock who spent his free time with Oxford rugby players and cricketers. Peter Levi was a noted poet with sidelines as an archeologist and travel writer. His brother Anthony was a fearsomely brilliant and ambitious scholar of French history. Vincent Bywater was an amiable don who would have been right at home in the Oxford of Charles Ryder, Sebastian Flyte, and the rest of the gang from *Brideshead Revisited*.

All these seeds of Ignatian-Jesuit formation took root and grew slowly as I worked as a reporter, corporate communicator, technical writer, magazine editor, and book editor, flowering in the late 1990s when I went to work at Loyola Press. George Lane, SJ, the genial president of the Press, hired me. In 2001 Jim Keegan and Jim Stoeger adroitly opened the Ignatian story to me and a busload of fellow pilgrims on a pilgrimage to Ignatian sites in Spain. A pivotal moment came a few years later when I made a retreat under the direction of George Aschenbrenner, a legendary spiritual director who played a big role in a renewal of the Society's ministry of **spiritual direction** in the years following the Second Vatican Council.

From then on, Ignatian spirituality became an increasingly large part of my life—personally and professionally. I worked with David Fleming, a gentle and reflective man, whose writing on Ignatian spirituality flowed with grace and insight. I collaborated with Michael Sparough and Tim Hipskind on a book about **decision making**. I was in the right place at the right time when **James Martin**, SJ, asked a colleague and me if Loyola Press might be interested in some writing he was doing. Yes, we said, and we published the best-selling book *My Life with the Saints*. I spent much time with Paul Campbell, SJ, a droll Irish-American-Brit, who was the publisher of Loyola Press. Because of Paul, I was present at the creation of IgnatianSpirituality.com, the leading online repository of Ignatian lore.

Today, my spiritual life (and much of my social life) revolves around St. Mary Student Parish in Ann Arbor, Michigan. This is a Jesuit parish that serves the students, faculty, and staff of the University of Michigan, along with a couple of hundred "resident parishioners" like my wife and me. I made the Spiritual Exercises under the direction of

Dennis Dillon, a poetry-loving parish priest with a doctorate in film studies from NYU (typical Jesuit, a friend says). Ben Hawley, the pastor, came to the Jesuits after a career at the State Department, and collected four advanced degrees along the way (another typical Jesuit). I've gotten to know Eric Sundrup, Michael Rozier, and Dan Reim during their stints at St. Mary's.

I spend time at Manresa Retreat House in Bloomfield Hills, Michigan. There I meet with my friends in the Detroit chapter of the Ignatian Volunteer Corps (IVC), including Leo Cachat, the IVC spiritual director, who spent decades in Nepal. It was at Manresa that I met Bernie Owens, a brilliant spiritual director with a mystical streak. Once Bernie was exasperated by a speculative and abstract discussion at a workshop on **discernment**, and he declared that "God isn't interested in 'what-ifs'; God deals with what *is!*" I often call this rule to mind when I find myself ruminating on the regrettable past or worrying about the possible future. It's one of the many gifts I've received from Jesuits.

Jesuits in Fiction and Film

Four movies featuring Jesuit protagonists are found near the top of every list of serious films that deal with religious themes. The most famous is *The Exorcist*, one of the greatest horror films ever. Who can forget the scene where the possessed girl, played by Linda Blair, spews pea soup in the face of the Jesuit exorcist? The other three are *Black Robe*, *The Mission*, and *Silence*. All three are historical dramas set in the seventeenth and eighteenth centuries in Jesuit missions far away from Europe.

The central theme of *Black Robe* is the clash of European and Native American cultures in French Canada soon after the Europeans arrived. The Jesuit "black robes"—so called by the Indians because of their religious habit—confront the implications of the native peoples' understanding of their faith that is vastly different from their own. *Silence,* directed by Martin Scorsese, tells the story of two Jesuits who secretly minister to persecuted Catholics in seventeenth-century Japan. The Jesuits' notions of sin and virtue are severely tested as they encounter a harrowing moral dilemma. My personal favorite is *The Mission*, loosely based on the work of St. Roque Gonzalez, set among the Guarani Indians in seventeenth-century Paraguay. It includes one of the great cinematic depictions of repentance and forgiveness, involving a Spanish mercenary and slaver, played by Robert De Niro, who does penance for killing his brother.

Three of these movies are based on notable novels. *The Exorcist* by William Peter Blatty was one of the great best sellers of the twentieth century, with some 13 million copies sold. *Black Robe* by Brian Moore was critically acclaimed, as was *Silence* by the Japanese Catholic Shusaku Endo.

Jesuits often appear in science fiction and mystery novels. *The Sparrow* by Mary Doria Russell centers around a Jesuit expedition to an alien civilization. *A Case of Conscience* by James Blish features a Jesuit priest probing the spiritual condition of an alien race. One of the religious groups in Frank Herbert's *Dune* saga is the Bene Gesserit, a powerful order with many similarities with the Society of Jesus (Gesserit = Jesuit).

A Jesuit named John O'Malley is the protagonist of the Wind River Mysteries by Margaret Coel, a mystery series set among the Arapaho Indians in Wyoming. Brad Reynolds, SJ, a Jesuit himself, is the author of the Father Mark Townsend mysteries, set in the Pacific Northwest and Alaska. Other mysteries with Jesuit protagonists are *Claws of the Cat* by Susan Spann, *Blood of the Lamb* by Sam Cabot, the Charles du Luc mysteries by Judith Rock, and *City of Silver* by Annamaria Alfieri. On her blog, Alfieri says, "If you want your priest character to be at once believable and at the same time have an unbelievable range of interests and talents, make him a Jesuit."

Jesus

When you walk the Ignatian path, you walk with Jesus. Ignatius was converted when he fell in love with Jesus, and his spiritual program is meant to help others love him too. Overwhelmingly, the Ignatian Jesus is a man of action. In the second week of the Spiritual Exercises, Ignatius proposes more than fifty Gospel passages for reflection and prayer. Almost all of them portray Jesus teaching and preaching, moving about, interacting with people, working to bring about the Kingdom of God.

Poverty is another feature of the Ignatian Jesus. Ignatius portrays Jesus as lowly and humble—a consequence of his mission in a world dominated by power, greed, and self-interested scheming. Jesus rejects these values and identifies with the poor and vulnerable. He empties himself completely to the point of death. He possesses nothing for himself but gives all to his friends.

Ignatius also sees Jesus as a friend and consoler. In the Exercises he says we should speak to Jesus like a friend, with great warmth and affection. He wrote to a group of Jesuits, "More than anything else I should wish to awaken in you the pure love of Jesus Christ."

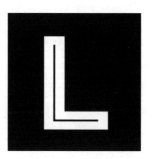

La Storta Vision

In November 1537, Ignatius travelled to Rome, full of doubt and uncertainty. He and his **companions** had been together for three years, resolved to serve the Lord together, but they had no clarity about what kind of **work** they should be doing. They had thought they should go to the Holy Land, but warfare between Venice and the Turks had made travel there impossible. The companions had temporarily dispersed into small groups to preach and do works of mercy in towns in northern Italy while they waited for a long-term solution. Ignatius decided to go to Rome to talk to the pope. He was wondering if he was on the right track.

He stopped at a wayside chapel in the village of La Storta on the outskirts of Rome, and there received a vision. In his *Autobiography* he says that "he saw so clearly that God the Father placed him with Christ His Son that he did not dare doubt it." He was looking for personal confirmation of his decision to go to the pope; this vision was it. Ignatius wanted nothing more than to be close to Christ. Now he was certain that he was.

But there's more to the La Storta vision. According to his friend Diego Laínez, who succeeded him as Superior General, God told Ignatius, "I shall be favorable to you in Rome." He understood this to mean that the upcoming visit with the pope would clarify the group's future. Laínez also said that Ignatius saw God the Father telling Christ that "I want you to take this man for your servant." In the tradition of the Jesuits, the La Storta vision led Ignatius to resolve to found a religious order and to call it the Society of Jesus.

Interestingly, the vision did not give Ignatius complete clarity about the future. He wasn't sure what God meant when he said, "I shall be favorable to you in Rome." He told Laínez that "perhaps we will be crucified in Rome." But instead of a glorious martyrdom, the companions received a warm welcome from Pope Paul III, who formally established the Society of Jesus three years later. Ignatius's uncertainty reminds us that even a mystical vision from God doesn't always give complete clarity.

Love

In the Ignatian view, love is always a verb. It's not a passive state but an active offering, giving, serving, and *doing*. In the Spiritual Exercises, love is always related to service. Our love for God is authentic when it involves giving of ourselves and making choices to serve God and others.

This notion of love begins with the nature of God, which Ignatius pictures in the **Contemplation to Attain the Love of God**. "God is Love loving," as the Jesuit writer David Fleming puts it, giving of himself, present in all things, laboring to make a better world, bathing us in an endless stream of gifts and graces. Our love is modelled on God's way of loving, expressed in the ***Suscipe*** prayer ("Take, Lord, and receive. . . ."). We give ourselves to God as he has given himself to us.

The Ignatian idea of love is summed up in two statements at the end of the Spiritual Exercises. The first one is: "Love ought to manifest itself in deeds rather than in words." There's a touch of hyperbole here; obviously loving deeds and loving words should go together. But the point is clear enough: talk is cheap. Deeds matter. Ignatius's second observation is: "Love consists in a mutual sharing of goods." Lovers share what they have with each other. In short, love involves *doing* things rather than *talking* about them, and the main thing that lovers do is to *share*. Love isn't one-sided; it's mutual.

Magis

Magis is an Ignatian buzzword. It means a striving for excellence, a determination to do more, an unwillingness to settle for the familiar. *Magis* is sometimes said to mean the greatest and the best, but the word simply means "more." Striving for the *magis* is about being willing to go deeper. Ignatian spirituality is flavored with the spirit of *magis*.

The word comes from a meditation in the Spiritual Exercises named **The Call of the King**. The retreatant is asked to imagine how he or she would respond to a call from Christ to join him in his work in the world. Most people would be happy to say yes; but for some, there's *more*:

> Those who wish to give greater proof of their love, and to distinguish themselves in whatever concerns the service of the eternal King and the Lord of all, will not only offer themselves entirely for the work, but will act

against their sensuality and carnal and worldly love, and make offerings of *greater value and of more importance.*

You can do what most people would do, or you can go all-in. You can ask to suffer the same abuse and rejection Christ suffered, and live in poverty as he did. Christ doesn't call everyone to this all-encompassing way of life, but the disciple of Christ can be *willing* to go this way. Someone who loves Christ will always look for new and better ways to serve him. As **Pope Francis** says: "The *magis* is the fire, the fervor in action, awakening those who have become dormant."

Everyone who experiences the Spiritual Exercises ponders the *magis*, so it's no wonder it shows up constantly in Ignatian circles. It implies a willingness to change, an openness to new ideas and perspectives. This gets expressed as a kind of restlessness. In 1995, the Thirty-Fourth General Congregation of the Jesuits declared:

> Jesuits are never content with the status quo, the known, the tried, the already existing. We are constantly driven to discover, redefine, and reach out for the *magis*. For us, frontiers and boundaries are not obstacles or ends, but new challenges to be faced, new opportunities to be welcomed.

Magnanimity

Magnanimity is a quality that Ignatius greatly valued. He wanted anyone making the Spiritual Exercises "to enter upon them with magnanimity and generosity toward his Creator and Lord." This is not an absolute requirement for making the Exercises, but it's close.

Magnanimity means having greatness of mind and heart. It's an ability to rise above self-interest and the usual worries about comfort and safety and choose the best thing, which may well be the harder thing. A magnanimous person isn't petty. He or she makes the extra effort—being the first to volunteer, walking the extra mile, giving someone your coat when they only asked for your shirt. **William A. Barry**, SJ, says that Ignatian magnanimity means having great **desires**. A desire to become more aware of God and to draw closer to him is what propelled Ignatius in his spiritual journey. That's what he wanted to see in someone who asked to make the Exercises—magnanimity, not theological sophistication, great learning, or deep holiness.

Magnanimity is the capstone of the Exercises as well. The culmination is the **Contemplation to Attain the Love of God**, a meditation on an infinitely generous God who is present in all things, laboring in love. The person's response is the *Suscipe* prayer—"Take, Lord, and receive all my liberty, my memory, my understanding, and my entire will, all that I have and possess. . . ." It's a magnanimous prayer. Those who say it understand that their deepest desire is to be a devoted servant of God.

Martin, James, SJ

When a big "Catholic" story breaks in the news, producers, journalists, and commentators usually call on a priest to explain things. These days, that priest is often James Martin, SJ, the telegenic author of many books and an editor of *America*, the weekly Jesuit magazine. Martin, who lives in New York, frequently appears on CNN, NPR, Fox News, and other media channels. He has written for the *Huffington Post*, the *New York Times*, and other publications. From 2007–2014, he appeared so many times on Comedy Central's *The Colbert Report* that Stephen Colbert named him the show's "chaplain." On Facebook, Martin posts a steady stream of videos, links, and comments about Catholic matters.

Martin's books *My Life with the Saints* and *The Jesuit Guide to (Almost) Everything* were both *New York Times* best sellers. He also wrote *Jesus: A Pilgrimage, Between Heaven and Mirth* (about humor in the spiritual life), and *A Jesuit Off-Broadway* (about his work as a consultant to a playwright and a troupe of actors).

In 2004, my friend and colleague Joe Durepos and I visited Jim when we were in New York looking for new authors for Loyola Press. Jim had written a few well-received books with modest sales, and he knew many writers through his work as an editor of *America*. He was definitely someone to get to know, so Joe and I took him out to dinner.

After dinner, Jim asked if we were interested in seeing something he was working on. Sure, we said, so he took us back to America House and showed us a big three-ring binder containing a manuscript. "It's a book about saints," he said, and he left us alone for a while to look through it. It took Joe and me about five minutes to realize that we had a great manuscript on our hands. It was about Jim's personal connection with sixteen saints, written in a lively, entertaining style. We thought it would sell very well.

Sometimes book editors misjudge how popular books will be. Not this time. Loyola Press has sold about 200,000 copies of *My Life with the Saints*, and sales are still strong more than a decade later. It's become a modern classic of popular spiritual writing.

Men and Women for Others

The Ignatian commitment to ministry to the poor, neglected, and marginalized is summed up in the phrase "men and women for others." It originated in a speech given in 1973 by **Pedro Arrupe,** Superior General of the Society. Addressing alumni of Jesuit schools in Europe, he called for a reorientation of **Jesuit education** to emphasize justice. "Our prime educational objective must be to form men and women for others," he said, "men and women who cannot even conceive of love of God which does not include love for the least of their neighbors."

In the decades since that speech, training "men and women for others" has become a paramount value shaping Jesuit education and Ignatian ministries. A vision of working for justice in solidarity with the poor is widely shared among those animated by the Ignatian spirit. It is doing God's **work** in the Ignatian way. It's the guiding vision of the Jesuit Volunteer Corps, the Ignatian Volunteer Corps, Ignatian Associates, the Ignatian Solidarity Network, the Jesuit Refugee Service, and hundreds of local outreaches to the poor, the homeless, immigrants, and young people. Lisa Kelly, a leader of the Ignatian Associates, writes:

Arrupe's vision articulated the blueprint for my life and the lives of many others—Jesuits, other religious, and lay—who have accompanied me, inspired me, taught me, and challenged me to do the loving thing in spite of a world that constantly instills fear. Today, some forty years later, I can't imagine there was a time when the word "Jesuit" was not synonymous with the word "justice."

Nadal, Jerome, SJ

Jerome Nadal (1507–1580) is probably the most important Jesuit you have never heard of. He was Ignatius's closest collaborator—the man he sent out to explain the Society's mission and spirituality, saying, "He altogether knows my mind and enjoys the same authority as myself." Nadal had an incalculable impact on the development of the early Jesuits. When they arrived on the scene, there was no precedent for a religious order whose job it was to be constantly active in teaching, preaching, evangelizing, and performing works of mercy. High church officials, and sometimes the Jesuits themselves, had trouble understanding who they were. Nadal was the man who set everybody straight.

His constant message to Jesuits was, "We are not monks." Monks stayed in monasteries, and other orders such as the Franciscans and Dominicans were based in settled communities. The Jesuits had no home. "The world is our house," Nadal insisted. He said that Jesuits "are in their most peaceful and pleasant house when they are constantly on the move, when they travel throughout the earth, when they have no place to call their own, when they are always in need, always in want."

Nadal summarized the distinctive qualities of Ignatian ministry in a Latin motto: *spiritu, corde, practice*, meaning "in the Spirit, from the heart, and practically." *In the Spirit*—**work** is done through the grace of God and with the conviction that God is in charge of it. *From the heart*—work comes from a heart transformed by Christ, and aims to bring about that transformation in others. *Practically*—work is practical and pastoral. This vision of Ignatian ministry is as fresh today as it was five centuries ago.

I especially love one thing he said: "For the virtues and good deeds of others, let there be sweet rejoicing; for the opposite, let there be only compassion, no judgment."

Like Ignatius, Nadal insisted that God is best found in the heart. "If you seek God in your intellect, you will become entangled in difficulties, and you will not find him," he said. "Seek God in the inmost movements of your heart, where he is found in serene quiet and sweet intimacy along with an unfathomable sense of his infinite energy."

Optimism

Ignatian spirituality radiates an optimism that distinguishes it from other spiritual programs and attitudes. There's a fair amount of tension and anxiety among people of faith: consternation over cultural trends, gloom about the prospects for the church, worries about rules not being followed, an apprehensive mood that focuses on what's wrong. By contrast, the Ignatian spirit is resilient and buoyant and filled with hope.

In his great book *The First Jesuits*, John W. O'Malley, SJ, says that optimism was an outstanding trait of the Jesuits from the beginning. He points to a couple of reasons why. Their ministry was centered on consolation; they saw themselves as "**helping souls**," and the best help was to lead people into a relationship with God. At the heart of their spirituality was **gratitude**. Twice a day they prayed the **Examen**, which begins with thanksgiving to a loving God who showers us with blessings and gifts. It's hard to sustain a gloomy mood when that's your prayer.

The optimism begins with Ignatius. When God caught his attention, he was an ordinary guy—an indifferent Catholic, a vain courtier with few prospects and a bad temper. He had scarcely given God a thought when God sought him out. Ignatius seems to have concluded that if God would speak to him he would speak to anybody, and he proceeded to develop a spiritual program to open people's eyes and minds and hearts to a God who is present in all things.

Howard Gray, SJ, one of the great contemporary interpreters of the Spiritual Exercises, says that Ignatian optimism is founded on trust. Ignatius learned to trust his own experience of God. He understood that God trusted him too; in fact, God entrusts his whole program of salvation to fragile and fallible human beings. Gray writes:

> Trust is the glue that holds Ignatian spirituality together—trust of God, trust of the process of the *Exercises*, trust in fellow Jesuits, trust in people's own experience of God, trust in God's presence in cultures, in learning, in art, in music, in technology. The litany of the objects of Ignatius's trust goes on and on. Ultimately, Ignatian spirituality trusts the world as a place where God dwells and labors and gathers all to himself.

Don't misunderstand; Jesuits can be negative, and sometimes Ignatian cheerfulness can morph into cloying naiveté. But the overall attitude is one of confidence. There's an assurance that despite setbacks and troubles, things are going to be all right and God is with us through it all.

Our Way of Proceeding

Baseball has a bunch of "unwritten rules." You don't flip your bat after a home run or steal second base when your team is ahead by ten runs. When you put the ball in play, you always run hard to first base even if you're going to be thrown out by a mile. It's all part of baseball culture—"playing the game the right way." The Jesuit version of unwritten rules is called "our way of proceeding." It's the Jesuit way of doing things, the Jesuit style.

It's an unpretentious style. By and large, Jesuits dislike formality and pomp (**Pope Francis** is a prime example). Most of them are priests, but they tend to adopt an "unclerical" style, shunning clerical dress and the clerical demeanor that separates priests from laypeople. Jesuits don't drive fancy cars, and most of them don't seem to care too much about how they dress. I remember when Paul Campbell, SJ, then the publisher of Loyola Press, bragged about a great deal he had found on eBay. He bought a bag of twenty used dress shirts for twenty dollars. He was wearing one of them; sure enough, it was a size too big and the cuffs were frayed.

The Jesuit way of proceeding is patient. Jesuits will tend to live with messy, ambiguous situations instead of plunging in and trying to clear everything up. Flexibility and adaptability are more important than rules. The Jesuit way of proceeding is shaped by the centrality of **discernment**. You reflect on your circumstances; you look for the movement of the Spirit. You wait for God to show up, and that means that you might wait a while, longer than is comfortable. The way of proceeding is a *way*—a journey, not a destination; a process, not a place. Ignatius signed many of his letters "The Pilgrim." The end isn't always in sight. What matters is moving forward in faithfulness to Christ.

In 1995, the Thirty-Fourth General Congregation of the Jesuits listed eight qualities integral to the Jesuit way of doing things. This is the most authoritative description of "our way of proceeding"—the written counterpart to the unwritten rules. A couple of items are specific to the Jesuits as a religious order: they are an apostolic body in the church, called to a "learned ministry," and committed to working with like-minded partners who are not Jesuits.

However, the other five items apply to everyone who follows the Ignatian way. They are:

- Being people with a deep personal love of Christ
- Being a **contemplative in action**
- Being in solidarity with those most in need
- Being people sent on mission
- Being ever ready to seek the ***magis***

"Permit the Creator to Deal Directly with the Creature"

One of Ignatius's most radical ideas is buried in the preliminary instructions, the **annotations**, at the beginning of the Spiritual Exercises. In the fifteenth annotation, Ignatius insists that the person giving the Exercises should never influence the retreatant in any particular direction. He writes, "The director of the Exercises, as a **balance** at equilibrium, without leaning to one side or the other, should permit the Creator to deal directly with the creature, and the creature directly with his Creator and Lord."

This was a surprising thing to say in the sixteenth century, when just about everybody in Europe was Catholic and expected their religious experience to be mediated by priests, doctrine, preaching, and devotions. It's still a radical concept. Jesus taught that each of us can have a personal relationship with God. Most important, we can *trust* our spiritual experience. God will speak to us, and we can hear him. We can open our hearts to God and find truth there.

This idea is at the heart of Ignatian spirituality. Because we can trust our spiritual experience, we can see where God is present in our lives. We can make good choices. We can live lives that bring us joy and bring grace to others.

This idea has also shaped the Jesuits and Ignatian ministry. In his book *The First Jesuits*, John W. O'Malley, SJ, says that the principle of permitting the Creator to deal directly with the creature caused the Jesuits to emphasize personal conversion above everything else. They worked comfortably and loyally within the church, but their program for renewal had little to do with changing church structures and reforming doctrine. The Jesuits didn't believe that right thinking about God would bring lasting change. Only conversion of the heart would. That's why they avoided church politics, renounced high church office, and concentrated on giving the Spiritual Exercises and "**helping souls**."

Not everyone agrees with the idea of the fifteenth annotation. Even people who agree with it sometimes backslide and wish for a spiritual system they can conform to. But the Ignatian view is clear: you will find God if you seek him. It's a truly radical idea.

Pilgrimage

The Ignatian metaphor for the spiritual life is pilgrimage. Pilgrimage is subtly different from a journey. The point of a journey is to get somewhere; the trip is something you put up with until you reach your goal. The point of a pilgrimage is the trip itself. You'll be surprised; you'll go to places you weren't planning to see; you'll learn new things, especially things about yourself. On pilgrimage, you don't settle down; you're always asking, "What's next?"

The pilgrimage metaphor comes from Ignatius himself. He referred to himself as "the Pilgrim" throughout his life, even when he was Superior General of the Society stuck at a desk in Rome. In 1522, after his conversion, he set out eastward from his family castle in northern Spain with the idea of settling in the Holy Land. Along the way he experienced profound changes. He abandoned strict asceticism, had mystical experiences, learned about **discernment**, and wrote the core of what would become the **Spiritual Exercises**. After his plan to settle in Jerusalem fell through, he returned to Europe and continued the purposeful wanderings that led to the founding of the Jesuits. He came to see pilgrimage as an image of the life he wanted Jesuits to lead. His friend **Jerome Nadal** said that the Ignatian way is a pilgrimage lived in imitation of Christ, "who had nowhere to lay his head and who spent all his years of preaching in journey."

There's an open-endedness about Ignatian prayer. **Imaginative prayer** typically focuses on Gospel texts showing Christ on the move. The **Examen** is a daily check-in looking for God's presence in daily events. It's a step on the pilgrimage. Hovering in the background is the question, "What's next?"

Pope Francis

"I think like a Jesuit," said Jorge Mario Bergoglio, shortly after he became the first Jesuit pope. Pope Francis has said and done many things that we're not accustomed to seeing from popes, and his Jesuit background explains at least some of them. Take, for example, his startling answer to the first question he was asked in his first interview. He was asked, "Who is Jorge Mario Bergoglio?" He replied, "I am a sinner." He elaborated: "This is the most accurate definition. It is not a figure of speech, a literary genre. I am a sinner." In other words, when I say I'm a sinner, I really mean it.

This answer comes straight out of the experience of the first week of the Spiritual Exercises. The meditations and exercises of the first week confront the person making the Exercises with the reality of sin: we are broken creatures born into a world deformed by sin. We are personally implicated in the evil we see around us. The lesson of the first week is that we don't know what redemption is until we understand our sinfulness, and we don't have much **zeal** for serving Christ until we grasp the urgency of his mission to save a ruined world. Pope Francis made the Spiritual Exercises twice in his life and meditates regularly on these truths. It's no wonder that "I am a sinner" sprang to mind when he was asked who he is.

Chris Lowney, a former Jesuit himself, views Francis through an Ignatian lens in his book entitled *Pope Francis: Why He Leads the Way He Leads*. He thinks Francis exhibits six qualities often associated with Ignatian spirituality. They are qualities held in tension, in three pairs. The first pair is a commitment to know oneself deeply coupled with a passion to serve others. The second is immersion in the world along with a practice of regularly withdrawing from it. The third pair is respect for tradition coupled with a desire for change.

When he meets with Jesuits, Pope Francis often talks about the Ignatian tradition. In 2017, addressing the editors of the Jesuit-run Vatican newspaper *La Civiltà Cattolica*, he proposed three Ignatian words as guides to the future, each accompanied by a Jesuit patron who embodied the spirit of the idea. I think his remarks apply to everyone looking at the world with an Ignatian cast of mind.

Francis's first word is *restlessness*: "Only restlessness gives peace to a Jesuit's heart," he says. "Do we have great visions and impetus? Are we audacious? Or are we mediocre, and content with laboratory reflections?" The patron is **Peter Faber,** "a man of great desires, restless spirit, never satisfied, pioneer of ecumenism."

His second word is *incompleteness*: "May your faith open your thought. Let yourselves be guided by the prophetic spirit of the Gospel to have an original, vital, dynamic, not obvious vision. Make Catholics know that God is also at work outside the confines of the church, in every true civilization," he says. The patron of incompleteness is Matteo Ricci, the Jesuit who brought the gospel and Western learning to China in the sixteenth century.

Francis's third word is *imagination*. By this he means **discernment**: "looking at the signs, listening to the things that happen, the feeling of people that know the humble way of the daily perseverance, and especially of the poor. The wisdom of discernment compensates for the necessary ambiguity of life." The patron of imagination is Brother Andrea Pozzo, a seventeenth-century Baroque painter and architect. "Life is not a white and black picture," Francis says. "It is a colored picture. Some colors are clear and others dark, some tenuous and others lively. This is the space of discernment."

"Pray as If Everything Depends on You"

One of the biggest tensions in life is between trusting in God and trusting our own talents and abilities. We need to do both, obviously, but it's easy to lose sight of one of the poles. Many people shove God onto the back burner and trust in their masterful selves. Many people make the opposite mistake; they assume that everything is in God's hands, so they don't worry too much about the quality of their work or training for it.

There's an Ignatian aphorism that gets at this problem: "Pray as if everything depends on you; work as if everything depends on God." We pray that way because what we do matters a lot. We want to get it right. It's entirely possible to get it wrong. We want to make sure that our actions are in tune with God's project. But once we make up our mind, we can turn the project over to God with complete confidence. It's not up to us anymore.

Interestingly, you sometimes hear the aphorism with the terms reversed: "Pray as if everything depends on God; work as if everything depends on you." That illustrates the problem: on one hand, an excessively "spiritual" over-reliance on prayer; on the other, a confidence in human effort that ignores God's grace.

Ignatius certainly experienced the tension between trusting God and trusting one's talents. God gave him mystical insights into things of the spirit; he wanted to help people experience the love of God for themselves. Yet he understood how valuable extended study and rigorous training were for people who wanted to bring the gospel to others. He completed an advanced degree at the University of Paris, and founded a religious order of men known for their brilliance and learning. But he insisted that trust in God always comes first.

The Presupposition

Ignatius operated in a religious atmosphere marked by conflict and suspicion. The Protestant Reformation was underway, and enforcers of orthodoxy were on the prowl. The words of teachers and writers were scrutinized and their motives were questioned. Ignatius himself was hauled before the Inquisition twice to explain his ideas. (He was cleared both times.)

When it came to the Spiritual Exercises, this pervasive atmosphere of mistrust presented a big problem. The director and the person making the Exercises had to be able to trust each other. The Exercises couldn't go forward if they were suspicious of each other's motives and wondering what they "really" meant. So Ignatius wrote a Presupposition stating a ground rule:

To assure better cooperation between the one who is giving the Exercises and the exercitant, and more beneficial results for both, *it is necessary to suppose that every good Christian is more ready to put a good interpretation on another's statement than to condemn it as false* [emphasis added]. If an orthodox construction cannot be put on a proposition, the one who made it should be asked how he understands it. If he is in error, he should be corrected with all kindness. If this does not suffice, all appropriate means should be used to bring him to a correct interpretation, and so defend the proposition from error.

In other words, assume the best. When you're troubled by what someone says or does, don't just give them the benefit of the doubt; put the best possible interpretation on the situation. Don't speculate about the person's motives. Don't wonder what he or she *really* means. If further clarification is needed, let the discussion proceed in all charity.

That's a pretty good rule for all kinds of situations. When your friends, colleagues, and family members speak, assume the best, not the worst.

Principle and Foundation

The Principle and Foundation is a short statement of about 150 words at the beginning of the **Spiritual Exercises** that sets forth the theological underpinnings of the Spiritual Exercises. In language that sounds a bit like the old *Baltimore Catechism*, it lays out a vision for human life. The first part of the statement answers the question, Why are we here?

Man is created to praise, reverence, and serve God our Lord, and by this means to save his soul.

The other things on the face of the earth are created for man to help him in attaining the end for which he is created.

Hence, man is to make use of them in as far as they help him in the attainment of his end, and he must rid himself of them in as far as they prove a hindrance to him.

The second sentence is the key; it tells us *how* we are to love and serve God—through the "other things on the face of the earth." Some religious traditions see the created world as an obstacle to holiness. Ignatius saw the world as the *means* to holiness. Thus, the choices we make in our everyday lives are just about the most important things we do. Here is the great challenge of life: choose the good (*"make use of them in as far as they help him in the attainment of his end"*) and avoid the bad (*"rid himself of them in as far as they prove a hindrance to him"*).

The second part of the statement is about how to make good choices that tap into our true **desire**:

> Therefore, we must make ourselves indifferent to all created things, as far as we are allowed free choice and are not under any prohibition. Consequently, as far as we are concerned, we should not prefer health to sickness, riches to poverty, honor to dishonor, a long life to a short life. The same holds for all other things.
>
> Our one desire and choice should be what is more conducive to the end for which we are created.

Indifference to created things means that we should work to achieve detachment when we make important decisions. The goal is freedom—freedom from fears, cravings, and anxieties that can distort our priorities. That, in a nutshell, is what the Spiritual Exercises are about—achieving the spiritual freedom to make the choices that will best satisfy our deep desire to love and serve God and other people.

Rahner, Karl, SJ

Karl Rahner (1904–1984) was one of the most influential theologians of the twentieth century. He believed that theology needed to find a way to express Catholic doctrine in terms credible to believers in a post-Enlightenment world. He worked to provide a modern philosophical base for the concepts of Christian revelation.

Much of Rahner's enormous influence is attributable to his vast output. He published some 4,000 works on virtually every theological topic. The basis for his theology is the idea that all human beings have a connection with God in any experience of meaning or self-transcendence. The ability to accept Christian revelation depends on this latent capacity to know God. This idea, which has obvious resonance with the Ignatian conviction that God can be found in all things, was viewed suspiciously by doctrinal watchdogs in the Vatican, who began an investigation of Rahner in the 1950s. But Pope John XXIII put an end to that by appointing him a theological advisor to the bishops at the Second Vatican Council. Rahner became the most important theologian at the Council; his influence can be seen in many Council documents, including *Lumen Gentium*, which declared that people who have never heard the Christian gospel might be saved through Christ.

Rahner wrote some beautiful prayers, including this one:

Thanks to Your mercy, O Infinite God, I know something about You not only through concepts and words, but through experience. I have actually known You through living contact; I have met You in joy and suffering. For You are the first and last experience of my life. Yes, really You Yourself, not just a concept of You, not just the name which we ourselves have given to You! You have descended upon me in water and the Spirit, in my baptism. And then there was no question of my convincing or excogitating anything about You. Then my reason with its extravagant cleverness was still silent. Then, without asking me, You made Yourself my poor heart's destiny.

Rules for the Discernment of Spirits

Ignatius distilled what he knew about good and evil spirits into twenty-two rules that he appended to the **Spiritual Exercises**. Ignatius never claimed they were complete, or that the spirits always operated the way he said. They are "rules" in the sense of "as a general rule . . ." They summarize what Ignatius had learned from years of experience reflecting on his own inner life and helping others pray and make choices to better serve God. They've stood the test of time. Today they are used intensively in Ignatian **discernment** and **spiritual direction**.

The rules are about identifying and interpreting **consolation and desolation**, Ignatius's words for spiritual states that signify the activity of good and evil spirits. He arranged the rules into two sets. The first set mainly concerns coping with desolation, that state of spiritual lethargy, sadness, and alienation from God that often afflicts us. The second set deals with false consolation—those **feelings** of excitement, confidence, and assurance that are produced by **the evil spirit** to lead us astray.

What follows is a summary of some of the wisdom in the rules of discernment that might be useful in everyday life. This is what I have found personally helpful. I don't claim to cover everything in the rules. I leave out details and nuance, and stay away from the subtleties of applying them. For that, you should consult the works of Jules Toner, SJ, and other Jesuit scholars and spiritual directors who have studied them extensively. If you want to use the rules for the discernment of spirits in making an important decision, the old warning applies: "Don't try this at home." Consult a trained Ignatian spiritual director for help.

Set One: Dealing with Desolation

The first set of rules is about combatting spiritual desolation. Desolation is bound to afflict us; this is how we handle it.

Desolation is normal. We're inclined to think that desolation is some kind of an aberration, a nasty interruption of the peace and joy that are the normal state of affairs in the spiritual life. Not so. Ignatius says that desolation is a normal state of affairs which we experience regularly. He views the spiritual life as a cyclical affair, with an ebb and flow of consolation and desolation reflecting the spiritual struggle in our divided hearts. So the first bit of advice is to stay calm. Don't let desolation upend you. Sit tight and wait for the feelings to change.

Don't make any big decisions. When you're in a time of desolation, avoid making big changes. This sounds like common sense, but people make big changes in desolation all the time. They break off relationships, quit jobs, write nasty e-mails, drop out of school, pack up and move to a new city. When we're feeling miserable, we want to do something—*anything*—to make the bad feelings go away. Thomas Green, SJ, a popular Jesuit spiritual director and author, says that we can avoid 90 percent of the unhappiness in our lives if we stick to this simple rule.

Do the opposite. Ignatius says that "in desolation the evil spirit guides and counsels," so it makes sense to do the opposite of what the evil spirit is saying. If prayer seems tiresome and pointless, pray more. If you want to isolate yourself, go be with people. If you're wrapped up in yourself, go help someone else. If you're restless and anxious, sit still and be patient and wait for consolation to return.

God isn't trying to tell you something. Another mistake—a common one, in my experience—is to think that God is sending you a message through the sadness and discontent you're experiencing in desolation. The supposed message is invariably negative: *This is my fault. God is unhappy with me. I have to do something different.* Remember Ignatius's rule: "In desolation the evil spirit guides and counsels." The evil one is doing the talking, not God. God may permit desolation, but he never sends it, and he won't use it to get your attention.

Master your thoughts. In desolation you can sink into a stew of apocalyptic thinking and dire possibilities. *This will never end. Everyone hates me. I'm alone.* Resist thoughts such as these, Ignatius says. Desolation takes away your **awareness** of God's constant love, but that love is always there. You will never be separated from it. God's grace is always sufficient to get you through times of trouble.

Use times of consolation well. When things are going well, decide how you will think and act when desolation returns. Your thinking will be muddled in desolation. You won't remember Ignatius's good advice to pray more, be patient, control your thoughts, and the rest. Remember it when times are good, and resolve to act accordingly when you're tempted to give up.

Talk about it. Don't keep your spiritual struggles to yourself. In fact, Ignatius says that the urge to keep problems secret comes from the evil spirit, who is not eager to have his lies exposed to the light of truth. Talk to someone who is skilled in discernment. Ignatius says that this should be a "spiritual person"—that is, a person wise in spiritual matters.

Set Two: Is This from God?

The second set of rules is about exposing those ideas, impulses, and desires that mislead us into making mistakes and bad choices. These are known as false consolations. We're excited, confident, strong—but these feelings may come from the evil one, not the Holy Spirit.

Examine everything. Ignatius observes, "It is a mark of the evil spirit to assume the appearance of an angel of light." This isn't surprising. You don't deliberately set out to do stupid things; every mistake seems like a good idea at the time. To lead a follower of Christ astray, the evil one needs to make a bad choice seem like a good one. No surprise, but this is also sobering, because you can't take your good feelings at face value.

It can be a thicket of deceit. Ignatius says that the evil spirit will "suggest holy and pious thoughts that are wholly in conformity with the sanctity of the soul." Then he will "endeavor little by little to end by drawing the soul into his hidden snares and evil designs." This means that your best thoughts and holiest desires can lead you astray.

Don't deceive yourself. Ignatius says that the evil spirit will propose "fallacious reasonings" to get you off track. This exploits the great human weakness known as confirmation bias: We decide what we want to do and then look for reasons to do it, ignoring warning signs and contrary arguments. It's important to keep an open mind, and be alert to the possibility that your hidden biases are distorting your judgment.

Beware of the fog of complexities and doubts. Ignatius warns of "subtleties and continual deceptions." He's talking about the thicket of misgivings, buyer's remorse, doubts, and sudden complications that emerge when you've set off on a new course of action. These are "*continual* deceptions"—they stick around long after you think you've banished them.

Pay attention to the "feeling" of the feeling. A false consolation from the evil one is likely to be noisy and disturbing. It's like a dissonant note in a pleasant melody—something jarring that doesn't quite fit. You're *too* excited. Your plan upsets your friends. You can't stop thinking about it. It's harsh—like "a drop of water falling upon a stone," Ignatius says. By contrast, God's consolation is gentle and delightful, like "a drop of water penetrating a sponge."

This is a taste of the rules for the discernment of spirits. There's a lot more that could be said about them. Think of them as a game plan for the struggle in the spiritual realm (which, of course, is no game). The first set is about playing defense; they'll help you fend off pressure from the enemy. The second set is about offense; this is how you avoid mistakes as you work alongside Christ in his work in the world.

Rules for Thinking with the Church

The rules for thinking with the church are eighteen statements about right attitudes toward the church that Ignatius appended to the text of the Spiritual Exercises. The most famous of them is Rule Thirteen, which includes the alarming words: "We must hold fast to the following principle: What seems to me white, I will believe black if the hierarchical church so defines." How could Ignatius, who prized spiritual freedom and warned spiritual directors not to tell people what to think, write such a thing?

First, we have to read the rules for thinking with the church in their context. They are not an integral part of the Exercises, but are added at the end, along with other rules for almsgiving, scruples, and the use of food. They are not for everybody, but only for those who might need them—mainly Jesuits who were operating in a religious atmosphere fraught with conflict and suspicion. We also need to beware of judging the past by the standards of the present. These rules reflect a sixteenth-century Catholic's understanding of the church. To our way of thinking, they seem exaggeratedly orthodox and excessively deferential to church authority, but no one thought so at the time. They expressed the conventional wisdom of the time.

As for Rule Thirteen—well, it says that Catholics should defer to the church when it says something that seems to contradict the evidence of their senses. This is what Catholics do every time they receive the Eucharist, which is the body and blood of Christ under the appearance of ordinary bread and wine. Much of the spiritual life involves holding fast to spiritual truths in circumstances that seem to contradict them. Rule Thirteen is not really such an outrageous thing to say. Ignatius phrases it flamboyantly, no doubt deliberately. It's a limit case—the far boundary. It's not the ordinary way to relate to the church.

Several of the rules deal with faith, grace, and predestination—the "hot button" theological issues of the day. The gist of Ignatius's counsel is caution and prudence: don't talk about these matters unless you have to, and be mindful of how easily what you say can be misinterpreted. It's good advice.

Society of Jesus

The name "Society of Jesus" came to Ignatius and his **companions** in 1537 when they were on their way to Rome for an important meeting with the pope. Their intention was to put themselves at the pope's disposal and ask him to give some official church recognition to their group. The question of a name came up: What shall we call ourselves? The answer came spontaneously: We'll say that we're the "Society of Jesus." The companions had long thought of themselves as a band like the first disciples, called by Christ to work with him. Ignatius had had a vision in a chapel in the village of La Storta on the way to Rome where he had seen God the Father placing him with Jesus, saying "I want you to take this man for your servant." Being known as Jesus' men—his "Society"—seemed right.

The name didn't sit well with some people. Religious orders typically took their name from their founders

(Franciscans, Dominicans, Augustinians, etc.). It seemed the height of presumption for this new group to claim Jesus' own name for itself. Some took to mocking the members of the new order, asking if they were "Jesus-like"—*Jesu-ita* in Latin. Thus the word "Jesuit" was coined—a derisive slur that its targets adopted proudly.

Spiritual Direction

Spiritual direction—the practice of one Christian helping another grow in a relationship with God—is central to the Ignatian experience. People make the **Spiritual Exercises** under the guidance of a director. Ignatian **discernment** is a collaborative project. From their earliest days, Jesuits have emphasized the importance of spiritual **conversation** and spiritual direction in the pursuit of personal conversion and growth in virtue.

In *The Practice of Spiritual Direction,* the Jesuits **William A. Barry** and William J. Connolly distinguish spiritual direction from therapy, coaching, counseling, and other forms of professional help. They define it as "help given by one Christian to another which enables that person to pay attention to God's personal communication to him or her, to respond to this personally communicating God, to grow in intimacy with this God, and to live out the consequences of the relationship." The focus of spiritual direction is the individual's relationship with God, which is most often experienced in prayer.

Ignatian spiritual direction emphasizes flexibility and collaboration. There's no pre-set program; the manner of the direction is adjusted to fit the person's personality, circumstances, and spiritual experience. The spiritual director eschews advice-giving and shuns the role of expert or guru. The director follows Ignatius's admonition to "**permit the Creator to deal directly with the creature**, and the creature directly with his Creator and Lord."

Ignatian spiritual direction is rooted in the theological vision of the Spiritual Exercises, which sees God as a giver of abundant gifts and graces, present in all things, and actively laboring to bring grace and light to the world. Ignatian spiritual directors typically focus on helping people uncover the deepest **desires** of their hearts. They make frequent use of Ignatius's **rules for the discernment of spirits** to help identify and interpret inner movements of the heart.

Spiritual direction has become a large and important Ignatian ministry. Most Ignatian spiritual directors are laypeople who have completed formal training programs at Jesuit retreat houses and spirituality centers.

Spiritual Exercises

"Spiritual Exercises" means two things. It's a book, written and revised by Ignatius over a period of at least twenty years, intended as a manual for spiritual directors. It's also a prayer-retreat experience, outlined in the book, which is intended to lead a person to conversion and a decision to serve Christ with renewed intensity and **zeal**. Everything about Ignatian spirituality flows from the Exercises—both the book and the retreat.

The book of the Exercises is a careful arrangement of material from different literary forms: prayers, meditations, step-by-step instructions, reflections, asides, rules, and notes. Ignatius began putting it together shortly after his conversion, which came about through reflection on the texts of the Gospels and lives of the saints. He made notes about these things, adding more observations as he reflected further on his inner life, learned about **discernment** of spirits, and helped other people grow in the spiritual life. The book eventually became a manual for a spiritual director helping someone through a spiritual experience like the one Ignatius had had. For years, Ignatius personally controlled the few copies of the book. He gave copies only to people whom he trusted, mostly men whom he had directed in the Exercises, for them to use to direct others.

The first printed copy was published in Latin in 1548, and many millions of copies have been sold since. It's one of the most important religious books ever written, but it's not a book that is meant to be read. It's a guide to retreat that's meant to be experienced.

The Exercises are arranged in four sections called "Weeks," which roughly correspond to four weeks of a month-long retreat. In the first week, the person does a thorough moral inventory; he or she confronts the reality of evil and sin, especially one's own personal implication in evil. The Exercises then turn to reflection on the mercy and love of God, who loved the broken world and the sinners in it so much that he sent Jesus to save it. The person making the Exercises is led to understand that he or she is a redeemed sinner, remorseful for his or her sin, but full of joy at having been redeemed by Christ. This is the essence of conversion. Many short Ignatian retreats are essentially experiences of the first week of the Exercises. The first week ends with the person praying before the Cross, "What have I done for Christ? What am I doing for Christ? What ought I do for Christ?"

In the second week, the person tackles the last of these questions: What ought I do for Christ? Is a change of life desirable? Is it possible? What direction might it take? The heart of the second week is a series of four meditations on the possibility of making a new or renewed commitment to serve Christ. In an exercise called **The Call of the King**, the person imagines hearing a call from Christ to join him in his work of healing the world. In another exercise, **Two Standards**, the person confronts the necessity of choosing a side: Christ or **the evil spirit**. **Three Classes of People** and **Three Kinds of Humility** consider the conditions for a decision and the lengths to which a disciple of Christ might be willing to go.

Christ's call is personal: "Whoever wishes to join me in this enterprise must be willing to labor with me, that by following me in suffering, he may follow me in glory." Accordingly, most of the prayer during the second and third weeks is reflection on the Gospel accounts of the life of Christ, employing a method of **imaginative prayer** whereby the person enters into the story as a participant or spectator. The idea is to observe Christ closely, to know him intimately, and to be like him.

In the third week, the person making the Exercises moves toward a decision. This might be a decisive change of life or something less dramatic—a determination to serve God in familiar ways, but with more zeal and fervor. Ignatius outlines different ways of **decision making**. Drawing on his own experience, he emphasizes the importance of discerning the meaning of the various emotions one feels while pondering an important decision. He gives twenty-two **rules for the discernment of spirits** to help the person identify the work of the Holy Spirit.

The fourth week is devoted to meditation on the glory of the Risen Christ. The final meditation is the sublime **Contemplation to Attain the Love of God**, which depicts God as present in all things, actively laboring to transform creation, bathing the world in blessings and gifts and grace. The person's response to this loving God is suggested in the *Suscipe* prayer—"Take, Lord, and receive all my liberty, my memory, my understanding, and all my will . . ."

Ignatius wanted the person making the Exercises to experience "great **feelings**": powerful emotions like grief, fear, **gratitude**, wonder, and especially **love**. The person is urged to take **desires** very seriously—to "pray for what I want," and to talk to Christ personally, "like a friend." The Exercises are meant to be a conversion of the heart, not the mind. Ignatius made this clear in the second of his **annotations** at the beginning of the Exercises: "It is not much knowledge that fills and satisfies the soul, but the intimate understanding and relish of the truth." This conversion is meant to lead to a decision to devote one's life to the cause of Christ—what Ignatius called "the election." This may involve a significant life change: a decision to enter religious life, to marry, to rearrange one's priorities, to do something very different. For many the election is not so much a turning point as a deepening of one's faith and a strengthened resolve to give oneself more generously in works of love.

In the annotations, Ignatius tells the director to adapt the Exercises to the needs of the person taking them. In fact, the director's proper role is to facilitate an encounter with God, not to manage it. The director "should **permit the Creator to deal directly with the creature**, and the creature directly with his Creator and Lord," Ignatius writes. Ignatius had an idea of how conversion of the heart could take place, but there were many ways it could happen, and many forms it could take. He wasn't rigid about it.

Over the centuries, the Jesuits developed many ways of giving the Exercises—ranging from the thirty-day "Long Retreat" to weekend retreats and parish missions. The Second Vatican Council reforms brought a renewed emphasis on bringing the **Spiritual Exercises** to a wide audience. The Society began to promote the Exercises, train laypeople to direct them, and develop new ways of giving them. Today the Exercises are more widely available than ever. The most popular form is the Exercises in Daily Life (also known as a "nineteenth annotation retreat"), in which the person goes through the Exercises over many months without taking time off from job and family.

Superior General

The Superior General of the Jesuits has broad authority to govern the Society and usually serves for life (although recent generals have resigned due to ill health or advanced age). In 2016 Arturo Sosa, SJ, a Venezuelan, was elected Superior General, the first not born in Europe.

The Superior General is sometimes called the "black pope"—black for the color of his "habit" in contrast to the white worn by the pope. The term took on sinister connotations in the sixteenth and seventeenth centuries, when it was used by Protestants and some Catholics suspicious of the supposedly vast influence the Jesuits wielded in the church. The black pope often appears in **Jesuit conspiracy theories** as the shadowy mastermind behind global plots.

The Jesuit **Constitutions** give a vivid portrait of the kind of person the Superior General ought to be. "Charity towards all his neighbors should particularly shine forth in him," it says. He should have "sound judgment" and "prudence along with experience in spiritual and interior matters." He should show a "genuine humility" and be "circumspect in speaking." He should show "kindness and gentleness" when making decisions that disappoint others. In temperament he should be **balanced**, "not letting himself be exalted by success or cast down by adversity." Above all, the general "should be closely united with God our Lord and be closely united to him in prayer."

The Superior General is assisted by an international group of fourteen General Counsellors. Nine of them are Regional Assistants, appointed by the Superior General, and four are Assistants elected by the General Congregation that elects the Superior General. One of the counsellors is an "admonitor," a confidential advisor whose job it is to warn the General when he is acting imprudently.

The Society is divided into eighty-seven geographic provinces, each headed by a Provincial Superior appointed by the General. The Provincial has authority over all Jesuits and ministries in his area. Each Jesuit community within a province is headed by a rector, often assisted by a minister who sees to day-to-day needs.

Suppression of the Jesuits

In 1773 Pope Clement XIV shut down the Jesuits. Colleges and seminaries were closed, lands and assets confiscated, and Jesuits were forced to renounce their vows or be driven into exile if they refused. It was a shocking affair. At the time there were about 22,000 Jesuits—more than there are today—and the order operated the largest network of schools in Europe. It's one of the most mysterious episodes in the history of the church.

The pope acted under pressure from the kings of Portugal, Spain, and France, who hated the Jesuits for various reasons. Jesuits supported the rights of native peoples in the Americas, angering colonial powers who wanted to exploit and enslave them. The Jesuits were allied with the pope, who was a secular ruler often at odds with the kings. They had assets their enemies wanted to get their hands on. And the Jesuits were not blameless. They played at the game of thrones at the royal courts and made powerful enemies. "There was much pride among us," one Jesuit wrote at the time.

Despite the pope's order, the Jesuits didn't go away. A remnant survived in Prussia and Russia under the protection of non-Catholic monarchs who had no use for the pope and refused to promulgate his orders. The political climate shifted. The French Revolution happened; the old monarchical order in Europe was swept away. At the beginning of the nineteenth century the pope was looking for allies to strengthen Catholic institutions, and he turned to the Jesuits. In 1814 Pope Pius VII restored the Society.

You'd think that an organization with such an embarrassing episode in its past wouldn't want to say much about it. Not the Jesuits. In 2014 the Society sponsored many lectures, seminars, and conferences about the suppression, to mark the two-hundredth anniversary of the Society's restoration. The idea, according to Adolfo Nicolás, the Superior General, was to "learn from the events, that we should discover the good and the bad in our behavior."

Suscipe

The *Suscipe* is a prayer of surrender at the end of the Spiritual Exercises. *Suscipe* is the Latin word for "receive," the fourth word of the prayer in English.

> Take, Lord, and receive all my liberty, my memory, my understanding, and all my will—all that I have and possess. You, Lord, have given all that to me. I now give it back to you, O Lord. All of it is yours. Dispose of it according to your will. Give me love of yourself along with your grace, for that is enough for me.

"Surrender" in a religious context can be a vague concept. Ignatius is quite specific: we surrender our liberty, memory, understanding, and will. There's not much left. God has given us these things; in the *Suscipe* we give them back to him. In return, we ask only for God's grace and the capacity to love him.

There are many prayers you can pray no matter how you feel. You can be in a black funk and still go to Mass; you can say a rosary when you're anxious and fearful. Then there are prayers that you'd better not pray unless you really mean it. The *Suscipe* is one of those prayers.

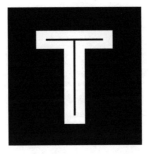

Teilhard de Chardin, Pierre, SJ

Pierre Teilhard de Chardin (1881–1955) was a French philosopher, mystic, and scientist, whose efforts to synthesize theology and evolutionary theory won him many friends but also got him in trouble with church authorities and his Jesuit superiors. Teilhard was a paleontologist and geologist who made important contributions to the study of human origins. He conceived a cosmic theological vision of creation evolving from primordial particles, through human consciousness, to a reunion with Christ in a future "Omega Point," which pulls all creation towards it.

Teilhard's timing was bad; he proposed his ideas at a time when church authorities thought that evolution wasn't compatible with an orthodox understanding of the Christian faith. His Jesuit superiors forbade him to teach and publish. He submitted to these restrictions obediently, and spent most of his life working as a paleontologist and trying quietly to explain his ideas.

Teilhard's books *The Divine Milieu* and *The Phenomenon of Man* were published after his death in 1955, and they gained a following. In 1962, the Vatican Holy Office issued a warning about the books, citing "ambiguities and even serious errors," but this turned out to be the high-water mark in anti-Teilhard sentiment. An effort to rehabilitate him soon got underway in the more open post-Vatican II atmosphere. One of Teilhard's most energetic defenders was the theologian Joseph Ratzinger, who quoted him frequently after becoming Pope Benedict XVI. **Pope Francis** drew on Teilhard in his encyclical *Laudato Si'*.

Teilhard's reputation among scientists is also improving. The idea that evolution might have a purpose is getting renewed attention from philosophers and scientists dissatisfied with hardcore scientific materialism.

You might say that all this posthumous respect was foreshadowed in a reflection Teilhard wrote in a letter to a friend:

Above all, trust in the slow work of God. We are, quite naturally, impatient in everything to reach the end without delay. We should like to skip the intermediate stages. We are impatient of being on the Way to something unknown, something new. And yet it is the law of all progress that it is made by passing through some stage of instability—and that it may take a very long time.

Three Classes of People

This is an exercise in the second week of the Spiritual Exercises that explores the idea of **indifference**. Ignatius believed that "we must make ourselves indifferent to all created things" in order to be free enough to make good choices. This exercise is a thought experiment that sets up a scenario that puts people to an "indifference test." It's supposed to make you think; it will probably make you uncomfortable too.

Here's the situation. You have three groups of people; each is given an enormous fortune of 10,000 ducats. (To put this in context, a university student in Ignatius's time could live comfortably for a year on fifty ducats, so this would be something like winning the Powerball lottery today.) All these people love God and want to do the right thing with the money. All of them realize that their attachment to the money is a problem.

The people in the first group talk about the problem of the money. They say they will consult God about it, but they never get around to doing that. They are all talk and no action.

The people in the second group *do* something. They come up with a plan to do something worthwhile with the money. But it's *their* plan. They decide what they want to do, and ask God to go along with it. "God is to come to what they desire," Ignatius writes.

People in the third group do what the others haven't—talk about giving up the fortune entirely. They can take it or leave it. Their only desire is to do what God wants them to do. This is indifference—the posture of complete freedom that Ignatius thinks we should strive for when making an important decision. Ignatius is not saying that giving up the fortune is the best thing to do. The group can keep the money or walk away from it.

The exercise invites us to look at our attachments. The problem isn't the money; it's our *attraction* to the money. So it is with all the things we love. How strongly are we wedded to our possessions, our career, our idea of the style of life we want to lead, our notions of how we want to spend our time and money? Can we walk away from these things?

There's a story about Ignatius that has to do with indifference. He once told a friend that the only thing that truly worried him was the possibility that the pope would suppress the Society of Jesus. "What would you do if it happened?" the friend asked. "I'd accept it," Ignatius reportedly said, "but I'd need fifteen minutes to compose myself. Then I'd be at peace." Ignatius's composure was put to the test in 1555 when Cardinal Gian Pietro Carafa was elected pope. Carafa didn't like the Jesuits. He had opposed the founding of the order and promised to suppress them if he could. Now he was in a position to follow through on the threat. When he heard about Carafa's election, a shaken Ignatius went to the chapel to pray. Six minutes later, he emerged radiant and peaceful, certain that everything was in God's hands. (Carafa didn't suppress the Jesuits, but two centuries later Pope Clement XIV did.)

Three Kinds of Humility

Three Kinds of Humility is a meditation in the second week of the Spiritual Exercises that explores the depth of commitment to Christ that a person might make. Ignatius uses the term "humility," but some who comment on this exercise suggest substituting "love." What kind of love do you have? How far are you willing to go with it?

The first kind of humility-love is to resolve to live a moral life in obedience to God's commandments. This is the minimum expected of Christ's servants. More is possible, but it should be noted that living a moral life isn't easy. It calls for a great love of God and a willingness to go to any length necessary to be faithful to God's law.

The second kind of humility-love is a determination to set aside your preferences and do only what would give greater honor to God. We strive for **indifference**: "I neither desire nor am I inclined to have riches rather than poverty, to seek honor rather than dishonor, to desire a long life rather than a short life." This is clearly a step up from the minimum. You want only what God wants. You imitate **Jesus**, who wanted only to do the Father's will.

The third kind of humility-love, the "most perfect kind," according to Ignatius, is to love Christ so much that you want to be poor and rejected as he was. You're not just detached from the riches and honors that most people want; you positively desire the opposite: poverty, dishonor, and humiliation. As Ignatius puts it, "I desire to be accounted as worthless and a fool for Christ, rather than be esteemed as wise and prudent in this world."

Ignatius doesn't say that anyone *should* seek this. Clearly, God must call a person to the third kind of humility; you would seek poverty and humiliation only after serious **discernment**. But some people do live this way. I thought of this exercise one evening when my book group was discussing *The Long Loneliness*, Dorothy Day's autobiography. Day exemplified this third "most perfect" way of loving. She had few possessions and lived as simply as she could, even when she didn't have to. She lived this way in imitation of Christ because she felt called by Christ to live this way. The third degree of humility is not *choosing* to live this way, but begging God to *call* you to live this way.

Deep humility, even of the third kind, doesn't mean passivity. Day was a fierce crusader for justice. She commented that she was willing to patiently bear wrongs done to her, but "we were not going to be meek for others, bearing *their* wrongs patiently." Ignatius was no shrinking violet, either. He strived to imitate Jesus in his poverty and lowliness, but when he thought God's works were dishonored, he responded fiercely. He defended his reputation from unfair attacks, several times hauling his opponents into ecclesiastical court to do so. He was a strong Superior General, determined to forge ahead against opposition when he was sure of his direction.

The Three Kinds of Humility exercise is intended to get you thinking about tough questions. How far am I willing to go in this "serving God" business? Should I be doing more? What am I holding back?

Two Standards

Two Standards is a meditation in the second week of the Spiritual Exercises that explores what it means to make a decision to serve Christ. It's an imaginative exercise. Imagine there are two armies gathered around standards, or battle flags. One army is led by Lucifer, **the evil spirit**, who sends demons out into the world to lead people to ruin through desire for riches, honor, and pride. The second host is led by Christ, whose disciples invite people to a life of poverty, rejection, and humility. We have to choose which standard we will follow. As the Bob Dylan song says, "It may be the devil or it may be the Lord, but you're gonna have to serve somebody."

The choice isn't as clear-cut as it might seem. Neither good nor evil is presented in their most obvious forms. Lucifer doesn't work through hatred, lust, and jealousy; he tempts us to riches and honor. These are not evil things in themselves; they can even be good. Similarly, Christ doesn't invite his followers to lives of kindness, mercy, and love as we might expect, but offers poverty, obscurity, and humility. These aren't necessarily bad things, but they're not very attractive either. In fact, they can be quite undesirable. Behind this schema is Ignatius's idea of how one thing leads to another in the real world. The path to ruin begins with the riches, moves on to empty worldly honors, and ends with pride. Christ also starts with riches, but he goes in the other direction. He invites us to poverty, which leads to rejection and ridicule, and finally humility.

Vice begins with "riches"—the "stuff" of the world: money, of course, but all the things that money can buy as well. It also includes intangible goods, such as our skills, reputations, and status. If this is what we value, we'll seek more of it—and more, and more. The problem isn't the stuff; it's the *longing* for the stuff. We get consumed in satisfying this longing. The end is malignant pride. The Jesuit Joseph Tetlow puts it neatly. At first we say, "Look at all this stuff I have." Then we say, "Look at me with all this stuff." Finally, we say, "Look at ME."

Virtue begins with poverty—not just a simple life, but also an **indifference** to worldly honors and status. Ignatius says that this leads to "insults and contempt." This is the consequence of opting out of the rat race; if we don't chase fame and fortune, we'll have less of those things, and those who have them get to think they are better than those who don't. This is how we achieve true humility. We are choosing Christ's standard. We're free of the illusion that we're at the center of things. Each of us has a part to play in the great drama of salvation, and it's not the starring role.

Uncertainty

Some very wise Jesuits who know a lot about **discernment** often speak of uncertainty. **Pope Francis** is one: "If a person says that he met God with total certainty and is not touched by a margin of uncertainty, then this is not good." Another is **William A. Barry**, SJ: "There is no guarantee that God will act in any given way with those who are trying to live the good life; one plants one's feet firmly in midair and marches on in faith, hope, and trust."

It seems that uncertainty is built into the nature of things. The Ignatian conviction that God can be found in all things means that no religious system is ever complete. We will never reach the end of "all things." Some things will always be hidden from us, and something will always come along to make God present in a new way. There will always be surprises.

It seems that the certitude promised by discernment is limited. We get a small peek at the mind of God; it doesn't come with a guarantee that things will turn out the way we think they should. Discernment doesn't give us certainty about the future. But we can have confidence that the decision we make *now* in these circumstances is the right one. We can trust that the **rules for the discernment of spirits** and other Ignatian insight can show us the way.

And we are free to make choices—truly free. I love a comment by a character in the novel *Mariette in Ecstasy* by Ron Hansen:

> We try to be formed and held and kept by him, but instead he offers us freedom. And now when I try to know his will, his kindness floods me, his great love overwhelms me, and I hear him whisper, "Surprise me."

Ward, Mary

Mary Ward (1585–1645) was born into the English Catholic aristocracy at a time when Catholics were being persecuted, driven into exile, and put to death. She caught the Ignatian vision from her tutors—Jesuit priests who were living in hiding in her home. She went to the continent and founded an apostolic community of women modelled on the Jesuits, a community in which women served in active roles in the Church. Her order grew rapidly and, throughout Europe, opened schools in which girls and young women were trained for teaching, nursing, and ministry to the poor and oppressed.

Ward's work met with considerable opposition in a society not accustomed to seeing religious women serving outside the walls of a convent or cloister. Her community was even suppressed for a time, but it was revived and approved by the pope in 1703. She is regarded as the foundress of two modern women's religious communities: the Congregation of Jesus and the Sisters of Loreto.

Ward advanced her vision of active women's ministry with fierce determination. She deplored the notion, advanced by some male ecclesiastics, that women's fervor would wilt because it depended on sweet feelings. "This is a lie," she wrote. Women can have fervor in aridity because "fervor is not placed in the feelings but in the will to do well, which women may have as well as men."

Work

In the Ignatian way of thinking, work is immensely important. We don't work just to pay the bills, to exercise our talents, to have a career, or to get wealthy enough to retire. We work for the grandest of reasons—"for the greater glory of God" (***ad majorem Dei gloriam***)—and for the humblest of reasons: **helping souls**. As **William A. Barry**, SJ, says, "Jesus did not give us a list of truths to affirm but a task to carry out."

In Ignatius's project, work is central. "Love ought to be expressed in deeds rather than in words," he says. He perceives God as a worker, present in all things, who "conducts himself as one who labors." He imagines Christ as a great leader, hard at work everywhere in the world, who invites each of us personally to join him. In the Ignatian view, we not only work *for* Christ but *with* him. The Call that Christ issues is to "work with me by day and watch with me by night," as Ignatius puts it in the meditation **The Call of the King**. Work is a path to holiness. We find Christ in the work we do. We become more like him as we labor along-side him, doing our part in his work of saving and healing the world.

This means that *all* work has dignity. All of it glorifies God if it's done freely, because it makes us partners with Christ in creating a better world. This is true whether we work in a warehouse or an office, whether we empty bed-pans or run the hospital. In fact, in the Ignatian tradition there's a great affinity for the humblest work. Ignatius him-self emptied many bedpans; he often worked in hospitals (dangerous places in the sixteenth century). He insisted that men entering the Society spend a lot of time giving humble service to the poor and sick—something that remains a big part of **Jesuit formation** down to the present day. **Jerome Nadal**, Ignatius's closest associate, said that "the Society has the care of those souls for whom either there is nobody to care or, if somebody ought to care, the care is negligent."

Ignatius once proposed a question to his friend Diego Laínez (who was to succeed him as Superior General). What would Diego do if given a choice between dying immedi-ately and going to eternal glory in heaven, and continuing to live and work with no assurance of salvation? Laínez said he would choose to depart for heaven immediately. Ignatius said he would choose to stay and do the work God had for him, "putting my eyes on Him and not on me, with no fear for my own danger or security."

Xavier, Francis, SJ

Francis Xavier was a star from the moment he showed up at the University of Paris in 1525. He was brilliant, rich, a scion of Basque and Spanish nobility, an athlete (his best event was the high jump), and fiercely ambitious. He was the youngest son in a noble family, so his path to fame and fortune lay through the church. He came to Paris to get a theological degree on his way to becoming a bishop or perhaps a cardinal.

Francis lived with **Peter Faber,** another brilliant theology student. In 1529, an older student named Ignatius Loyola moved into their boarding house. He was an odd character, fifteen years their senior and a former soldier with a burning desire to serve Christ. At first Francis wasn't impressed with Ignatius at all; he made jokes about his efforts to convert students. But over time Francis warmed up to Ignatius and became one of his closest friends. He was one of the seven **companions** who formed the nucleus of the Jesuits.

Xavier was a natural leader with a charismatic personality. It is thought that Ignatius was grooming him to succeed him as Superior General. But in 1540 a Jesuit who had been appointed to lead a missionary journey to the Portuguese possessions in India fell ill, and Ignatius appointed Francis to replace him. He left Europe in 1541, never to return. He travelled to Mozambique, Goa, Malaysia, and Japan, spreading the Catholic faith and becoming the most famous missionary in history. He died in 1552 as he was preparing to enter China.

Xavier more than Ignatius gets the credit for the phenomenal growth of the early Jesuits. His letters home were widely circulated in Europe, and they inspired many young men to join the Jesuits hoping to follow in his footsteps. Here's an excerpt from a letter Xavier sent to his companions in Rome in 1544:

> Many times I am seized with the thought of going to the schools in your lands and crying out there, like a man who has lost his mind, and especially at the University of Paris, telling those in the Sorbonne who have greater regard for learning than desire to prepare themselves to produce fruit with it: "How many souls fail

to go to glory and go instead to hell through their neglect!"

Xavier deeply loved Ignatius and his other friends in the Society, and he missed them terribly. In a poignant letter, he tells them that he has cut their names out of letters they have written him so he can carry them with him at all times.

Z

Zeal

Z is for zeal—a good word for the end of the Ignatian alphabet. The Ignatian spirit is zealous—intense, avid, keen to move ahead. At the heart of the Ignatian experience is the longing for *magis*—"more," the better choice, the more excellent way. But how do we sustain zeal? This is the perpetual challenge facing movements born of religious awakenings. Without constant renewal, zealous people burn out and zealous organizations slowly sink into mediocrity.

This is the problem that **Pope Francis** talked about at the Thirty-Sixth General Congregation of the Jesuits in 2016. It was a big moment. General Congregations happen infrequently—there have only been thirty-six of them in five centuries. On these occasions representatives of the whole Society gather to discuss problems and to set the course for the future. And so we might expect the words of a Jesuit pope to such a gathering to have special weight. What

Francis said isn't limited to the Jesuits, but applies to everyone who walks the Ignatian way.

The first remedy for flagging zeal is "to ask insistently for consolation." In *The First Jesuits*, John W. O'Malley, SJ, writes that consolation marked the ministries of the early Jesuits. They sought to bring people the interior joy that comes with a relationship with God. Francis reminds the Jesuits of this history and urges them to "remain persistent in prayer for consolation," and to teach people how to pray that way. He points to the Spiritual Exercises as the "method par excellence" for finding the graces of consolation.

The second route to renewed zeal is embracing the cross—"letting ourselves be moved by the Lord crucified," Francis says. This means facing our own wounds and brokenness so that we can receive God's mercy. Francis points to the example of Ignatius, who rejoiced in his faults and sins precisely because this made him aware of how God had so lavishly blessed him. From the experience of God's mercy comes the capacity to show mercy to others—"to the poorest, to sinners, to those discarded people, and those crucified in the present world, who suffer injustice and violence." It brings solidarity—"We hasten to walk patiently with our people, learning from them the best way of helping and serving them."

The third prescription for renewal is to employ **discernment**. Don't just make plans or organize projects, but "recollect oneself before talking and acting in order to work in the Good Spirit." Operating in a spirit of discernment means thinking with the church. This has a specific ecclesial meaning for the Jesuits, who are an order in the church; for everyone walking the Ignatian path it means operating in concert with others.

Consolation, compassion, discernment—these are the ways to sustain and renew our zeal to work with Christ in his mission to heal a broken world. I give Francis, the first Jesuit pope, the last word on Ignatian spirituality:

> We neither walk alone nor comfortably, but we walk with a heart that does not rest, that does not close in on itself but beats to the rhythm of a journey undertaken together with all the people faithful to God.

An Ignatian Reading List

Here are some books and other resources that can help you on your Ignatian journey. This is my personal selection of the best of a vast library of material about Ignatian spirituality and Jesuit history.

Ignatian Prayer 101

Getting started on the Ignatian path means developing a habit of prayer.

A Simple Life-Changing Prayer: Discovering the Power of St. Ignatius Loyola's Examen by Jim Manney (Chicago: Loyola Press, 2011). The Daily Examen is the gateway into Ignatian spirituality.

An Ignatian Book of Days, compiled by Jim Manney (Chicago: Loyola Press, 2014). 365 selections from the Ignatian tradition for daily prayer and reflection.

Pray as You Go (**https://pray-as-you-go.org**)

Sacred Space Daily Prayer (**www.sacredspace.ie**)
These smartphone apps from Jesuit ministries offer daily
prayer with an Ignatian flavor.

Going Deeper into Ignatian Prayer

Two books by William A. Barry, SJ, and one by Tim
Muldoon:

God and You: Prayer as a Personal Relationship (Mahwah, NJ:
Paulist, 1987).

*A Friendship Like No Other: Experiencing God's Amazing
Embrace* (Chicago: Loyola Press, 2008).

*The Ignatian Workout: Daily Spiritual Exercises for a Healthy
Faith* by Tim Muldoon (Chicago: Loyola Press, 2004).

Learning More about Ignatian Spirituality

Three books and one website for more study:

The Jesuit Guide to (Almost) Everything by James Martin, SJ.
(San Francisco: Harper One, 2012). A big, well-written
book full of good information and sound advice.

IgnatianSpirituality.com (Loyola Press) A comprehensive
online resource with material on virtually every
Ignatian topic.

What Is Ignatian Spirituality? by David L. Fleming, SJ
(Chicago: Loyola Press, 2008). Twenty short chapters on key
Ignatian ideas.

*Discovering Your Dream: How Ignatian Spirituality Can
Guide your Life* by Gerald M. Fagin, SJ (Chicago: Loyola
Press, 2013). A short book that is especially popular with
college students and young adults.

Learning Even More

Four books that delve more deeply into Ignatian spirituality
and the Jesuit world:

Contemplatives in Action: The Jesuit Way by William A.
Barry, SJ, and Robert G. Doherty, SJ (Mahwah, NJ: Paulist,
2005). The Ignatian charism is to hold apparently opposing
values and ideas in balance.

*Heroic Leadership: Best Practices from a 450-Year-Old
Company That Changed the World* by Chris Lowney
(Chicago: Loyola Press, 2005). Leadership lessons and values
for living drawn from the history of the Jesuits.

An Ignatian Spirituality Reader, edited by George Traub, SJ
(Chicago: Loyola Press, 2005). See especially the essays on
Ignatius by Ron Hansen, on finding God in all things by
Monika Hellwig, on Ignatian spirituality by Howard
Gray, SJ, and on the Examen by Dennis Hamm, SJ.

Eyes to See, Ears to Hear: An Introduction to Ignatian Spirituality by David Lonsdale (Maryknoll, NY: Orbis Books, 2000). See especially his chapters on Ignatian prayer and discernment of spirits.

The Spiritual Exercises

Translations

For this book, I used the translation by Louis Puhl, SJ (Chicago: Loyola Press, 1968), available online at **spex.ignatianspirituality.com**.

Draw Me into Your Friendship by David L. Fleming, SJ (St. Louis: Institute of Jesuit Resources, 1996). A paraphrase of the Exercises in contemporary language published on facing pages with a translation by Eldar Mullen, SJ.

Making the Exercises

Two books for praying through the Exercises yourself:

The Ignatian Adventure: Experiencing the Spiritual Exercises of St. Ignatius in Daily Life by Kevin O'Brien, SJ (Chicago: Loyola Press, 2011).

Retreat in the Real World: Finding Intimacy with God Wherever You Are by Andy Alexander, SJ, Maureen McCann Waldron, and Larry Gillick, SJ (Chicago: Loyola Press, 2008). This book is based on a retreat from Creighton

University Online Ministries and published at
onlineministries.creighton.edu.

Making the Exercises with a spiritual director

Three books about the Exercises that will give you an idea of
what you'd be getting into:

*Stretched for Greater Glory: What to Expect from the Spiritual
Exercises* by George Aschenbrenner, SJ (Chicago: Loyola
Press, 2004).

*Finding God in All Things: A Companion to the Spiritual
Exercises of St. Ignatius* by William A. Barry, SJ (Notre Dame,
IN: Ave Maria Press, 2009).

God Finds Us: An Experience of the Spiritual Exercises by Jim
Manney (Chicago: Loyola Press, 2013).

Studying the Spiritual Exercises

Understanding the Spiritual Exercises by Michael Ivens, SJ
(Herefordshire, England: Gracewing, 2016). Commentary
on the Exercises and the Rules for the Discernment of Spirits
by a noted scholar.

Commentary about the Exercises can be found at
spex.ignatianspirituality.com.

Ignatius and Jesuit History

Saint Ignatius' Own Story translated by William J. Young, SJ (Chicago: Loyola Press, 1982). Ignatius's autobiography with a sampling of his letters.

Ignatius Loyola: A Biography of the Founder of the Jesuits by Philip Caraman, SJ (San Francisco: HarperCollins, 1990). A well-written biography of the saint.

The First Jesuits by John W. O'Malley, SJ (Cambridge, MA: Harvard University Press, 1993). A monumental and award-winning study.

Ignatian Humanism: A Dynamic Spirituality for the 21st Century by Ronald Modras (Chicago: Loyola Press, 2004). Explores the humanist underpinnings of Ignatian education and ministry.

The Ignatian Tradition by Kevin F. Burke, SJ and Eileen Burke-Sullivan (Collegeville, MN: Liturgical Press, 2009). Portraits of Jesuits through the ages and excerpts from their writings.

Discernment

Practicing discernment

Two books for understanding Ignatian discernment:

What Do You Really Want? St. Ignatius Loyola and the Art of Discernment by Jim Manney (Huntington, IN: Our Sunday Visitor, 2015).

God's Voice Within: The Ignatian Way to Discover God's Will by Mark Thibodeaux, SJ (Chicago: Loyola Press, 2010).

Studying discernment

For spiritual directors and others who want to delve deeper:

The Discernment of Spirits by Timothy M. Gallagher, OMV (Spring Valley, NY: Crossroad, 2005).

The books of Jules Toner, SJ, all published by the Institute of Jesuit Sources at Boston College, Boston, MA.

A Commentary on St. Ignatius's Rules for the Discernment of Spirits

Discerning God's Will: Ignatius of Loyola's Teaching on Christian Decision Making

Spirit of Light or Darkness? A Casebook for Studying Discernment of Spirits

What Is Your Will O God? A Casebook for Studying Discernment of God's Will

Spiritual Direction

The Practice of Spiritual Direction by William A. Barry, SJ, and William J. Connolly, SJ (San Francisco: Harper One, 2009).

Spiritual Direction and the Encounter with God: A Theological Inquiry by William A. Barry, SJ (Mahwah, NJ: Paulist Press, 2005).

Pope Francis

Two books that show the Ignatian side of the Jesuit pope:

Pope Francis: Why He Leads the Way He Leads by Chris Lowney (Chicago: Loyola Press, 2013).

The Church of Mercy: A Vision for the Church by Pope Francis (Chicago: Loyola Press, 2014).

Special Mention

Two great books by Jesuit authors:

My Life with the Saints by James Martin, SJ (Chicago: Loyola Press, 2007). A modern spiritual classic.

Tattoos on the Heart: The Power of Boundless Compassion by Gregory Boyle, SJ (New York City: Free Press, 2011). Marvelous stories and reflections by a Jesuit who works with gangs in East Los Angeles.

Acknowledgments

I owe a debt of gratitude to my friends at Loyola Press for their help on this book. Joe Durepos proposed it, honed the concept, and made many invaluable comments and suggestions. Vinita Wright, Mary Collins, and Patrice Tuohy did wonderful work on the manuscript. I'm grateful to Tom McGrath and Terry Locke for their support. They've made Loyola Press the premier publisher of Ignatian material.

Thanks to my friends Etta MacDonagh-Dumler, Ben Hawley, SJ, and William Barry, SJ, for their help and ideas. And special thanks to my wife, Susan, my best reader.

About the Author

Jim Manney is the author of highly praised popular books on Ignatian spirituality, including *A Simple, Life-Changing Prayer* (about the Daily Examen), *God Finds Us* (about the Spiritual Exercises), and *What Do You Really Want?* (about discernment). He is the compiler/editor of the acclaimed *An Ignatian Book of Days.* For many years he was senior editor at Loyola Press, where he was founding editor of Ignatian-Spirituality.com and a long-time contributor to the dot-Magis blog. Jim and his wife live in Ann Arbor, Michigan.

Other Ignatian Titles

What Is Ignatian Spirituality?
David Fleming, SJ
ENGLISH | 2718-9 | PB | $12.95
SPANISH | 3883-3 | PB | $12.95

Jesuits Telling Jokes
Nikolaas Sintobin, SJ
4373-8 | PB | $10.95

Hearts on Fire
Michael Harter, SJ
2120-3 | PB | $12.95

The Ignatian Adventure
Kevin O'Brien, SJ
ENGLISH | 3577-1 | PB | $14.95
SPANISH | 4520-6 | PB | $14.95

Reimagining the Ignatian Examen
Mark E. Thibodeaux, SJ
ENGLISH | 4244-1 | PB | $12.95
SPANISH | 4512-1 | PB | $12.95

To Order:

Call **800.621.1008**, visit **loyolapress.com/store**, or visit your local bookseller.

Also By **Jim Manney**

A Simple, Life-Changing Prayer

Discovering the Power of St. Ignatius Loyola's Examen

ENGLISH | 3535-1 | PB | $9.95
SPANISH | 4389-9 | PB | $9.95

What's Your Decision?

How to Make Choices with Confidence and Clarity

3148-3 | PB | $10.95

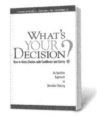

An Ignatian Book of Days

4145-1 | PB | $12.95

God Finds Us

An Experience of the Spiritual Exercises of St. Ignatius Loyola

3827-7 | PB | $9.95

To Order:

Call **800.621.1008**, visit **loyolapress.com/store**, or visit your local bookseller.

Ignatian Spirituality
www.ignatianspirituality.com

Visit us online to

- Join our E-Magis newsletter
- Pray the Daily Examen
- Make an online retreat with the *Ignatian Prayer Adventure*
- Participate in the conversation with the dotMagis blog and at **facebook.com/ignatianspirituality**